To all the young champions,

May this coloring book inspire you to reach for the stars, just like the athletes of the 2024 Olympics. Let your colors shine as brightly as your dreams, and may every page fill your heart with the Olympic spirit of determination, unity, and joy.

With love and Olympic dreams.

This book belongs to:

_____

Copyright Reserved

© 2024 by Dre Florio

All rights reserved. No part of this coloring book may be reproduced, stored in a retrieval system, or transmitted in any form or by any means, electronic, mechanical, photocopying, recording, or otherwise, without the prior written permission of the copyright holder.

This book was created with love and care to inspire children's creativity. We hope you enjoy coloring each page and bringing the illustrations to life!

Remember: imagination knows no bounds!

Araucária Publications

Test color page

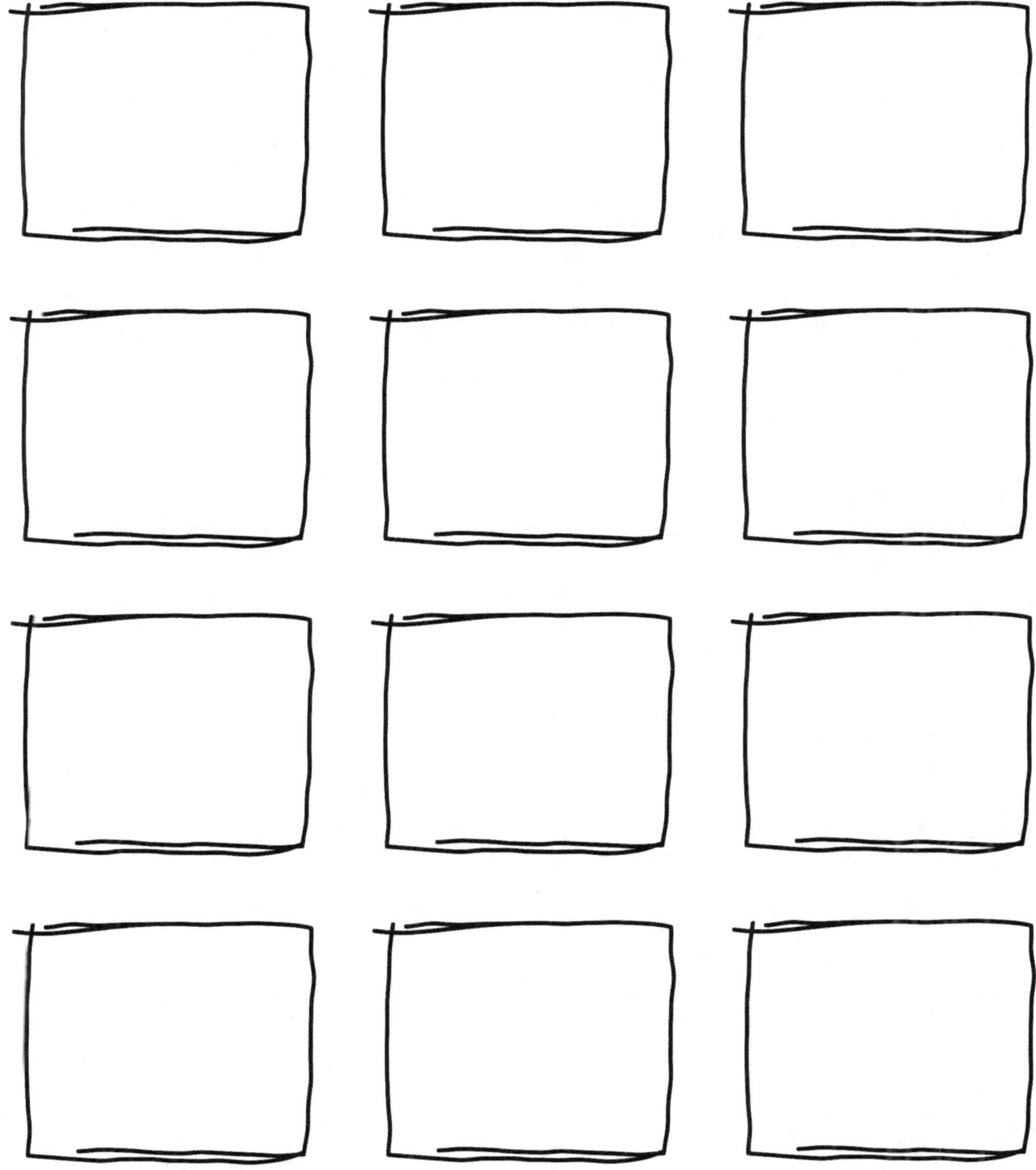

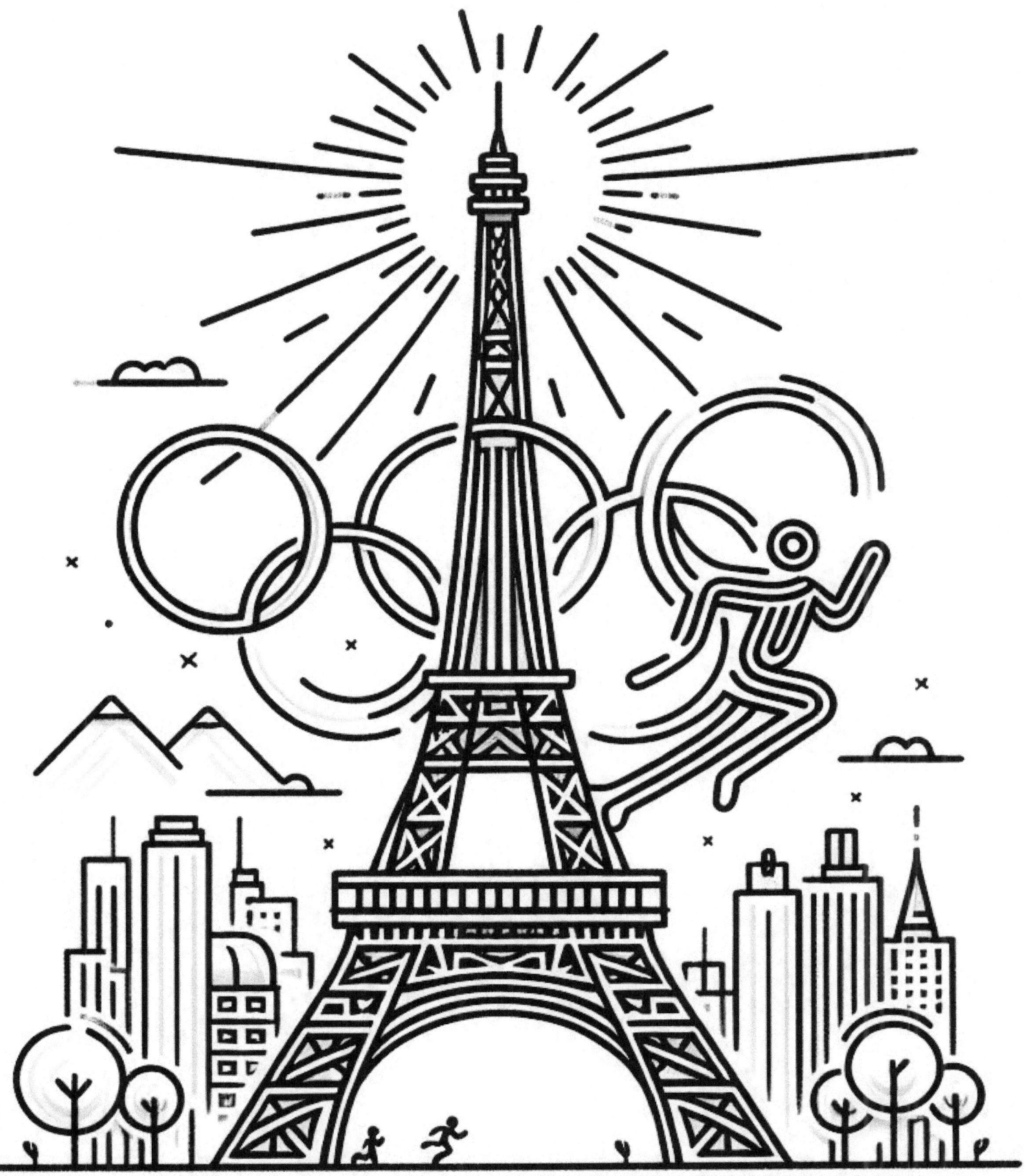

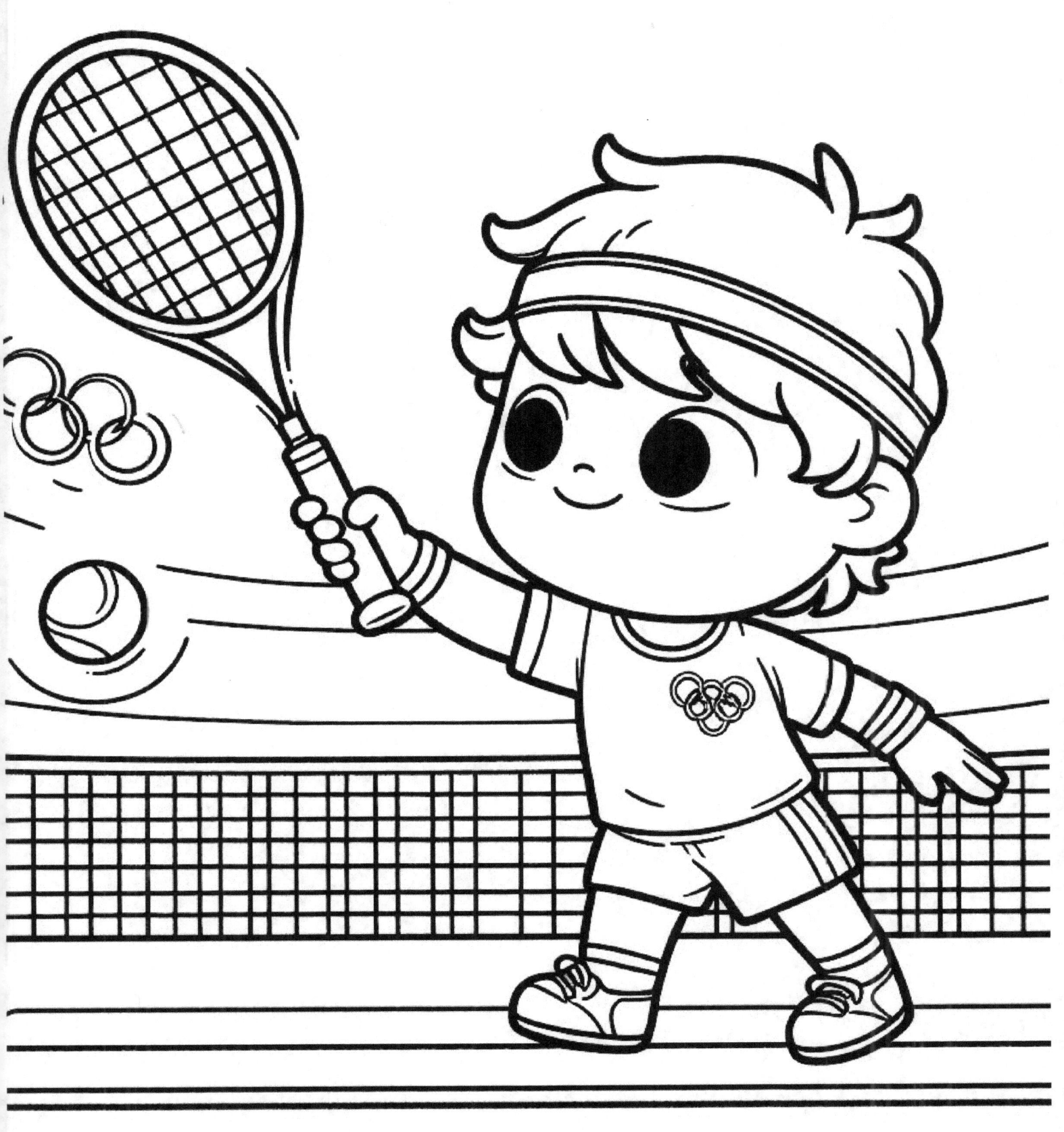

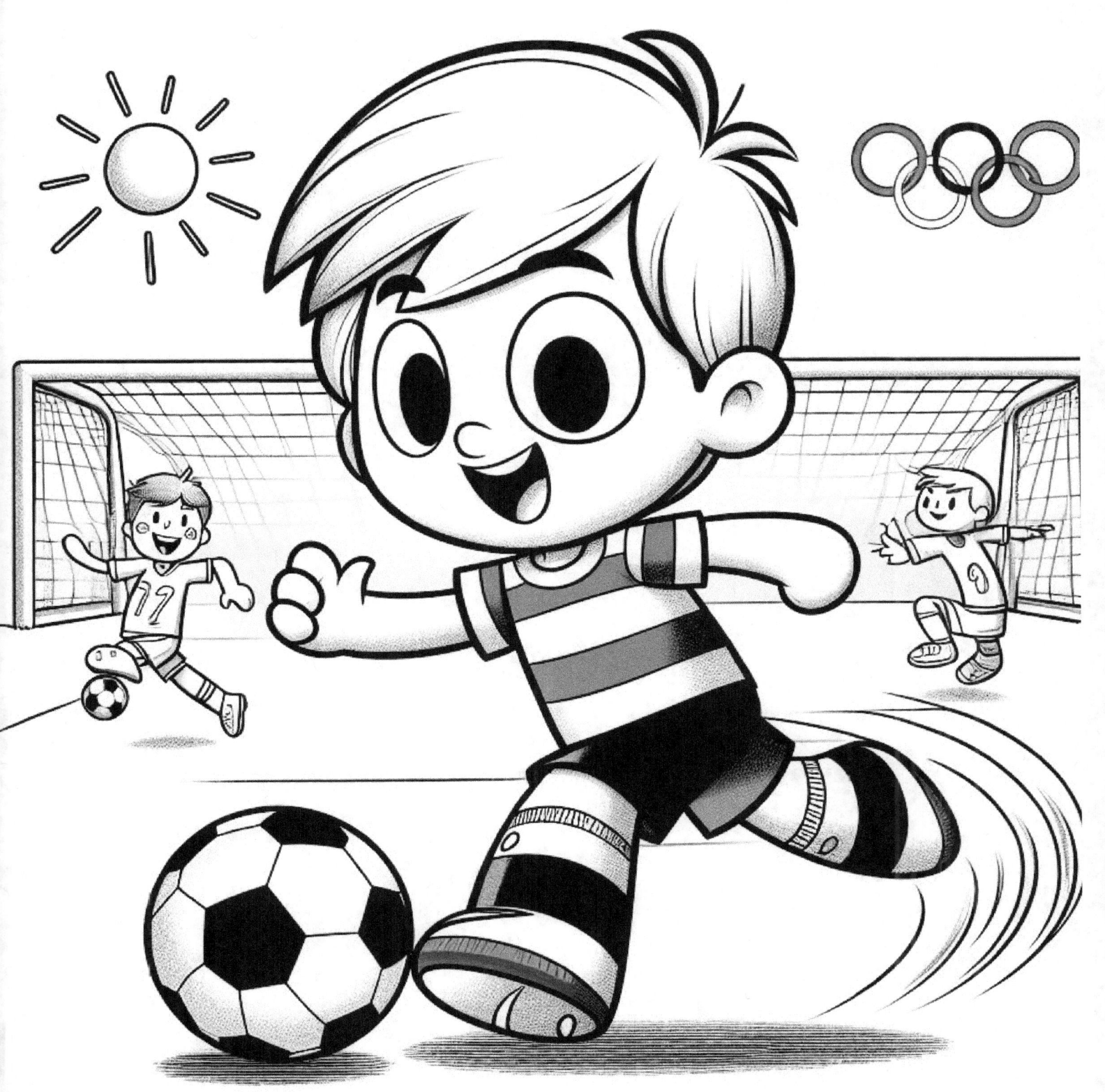

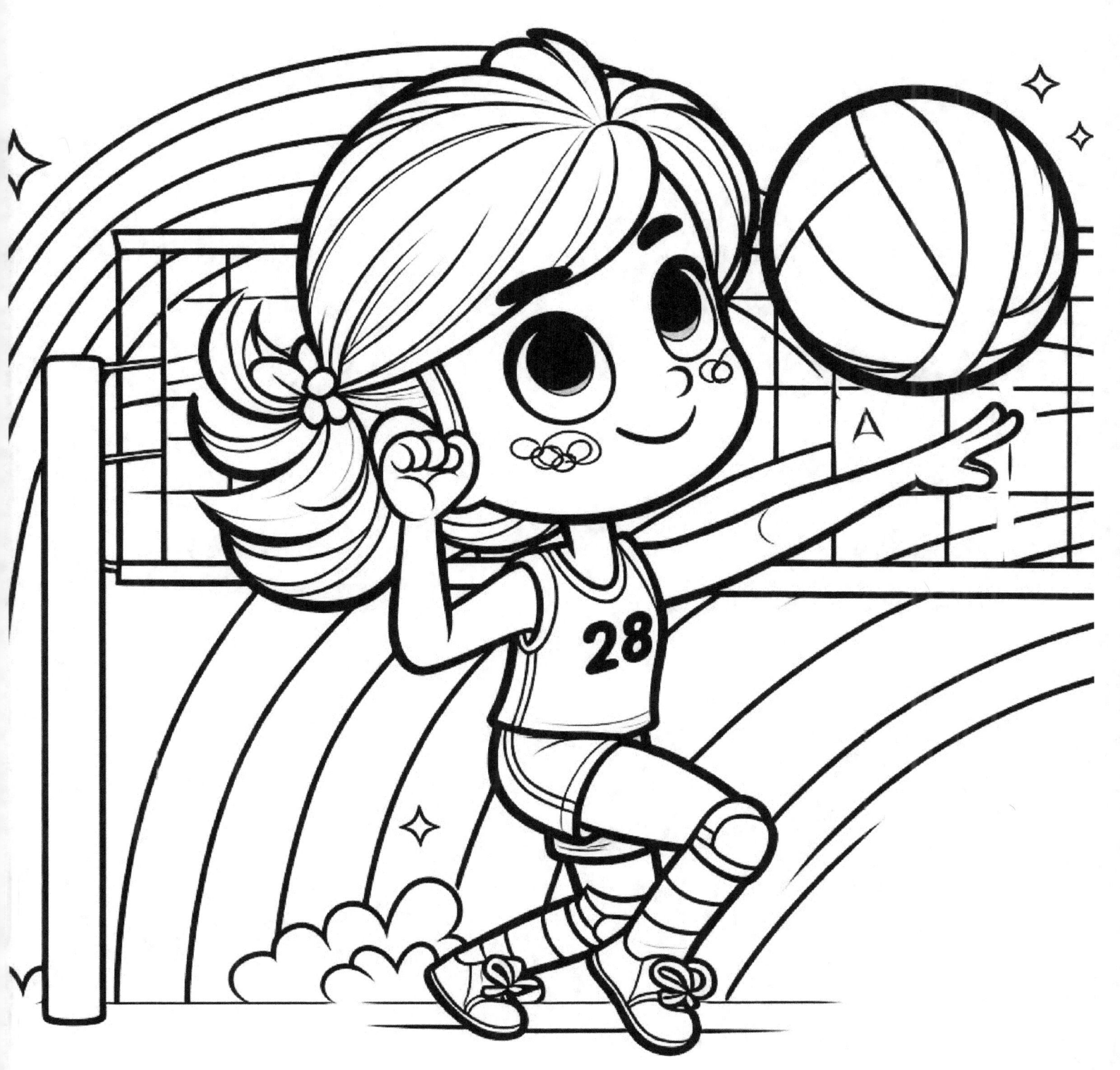

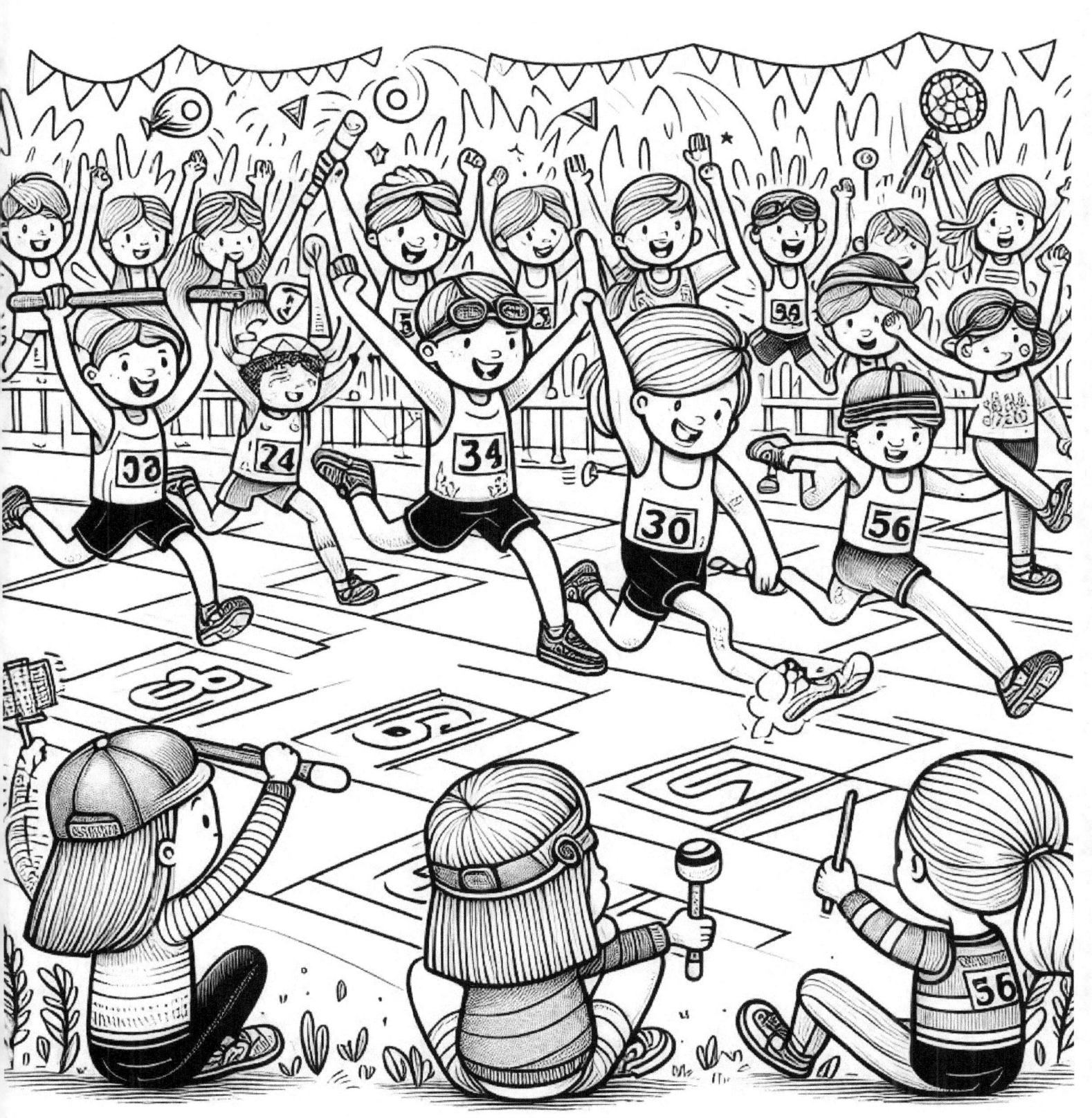

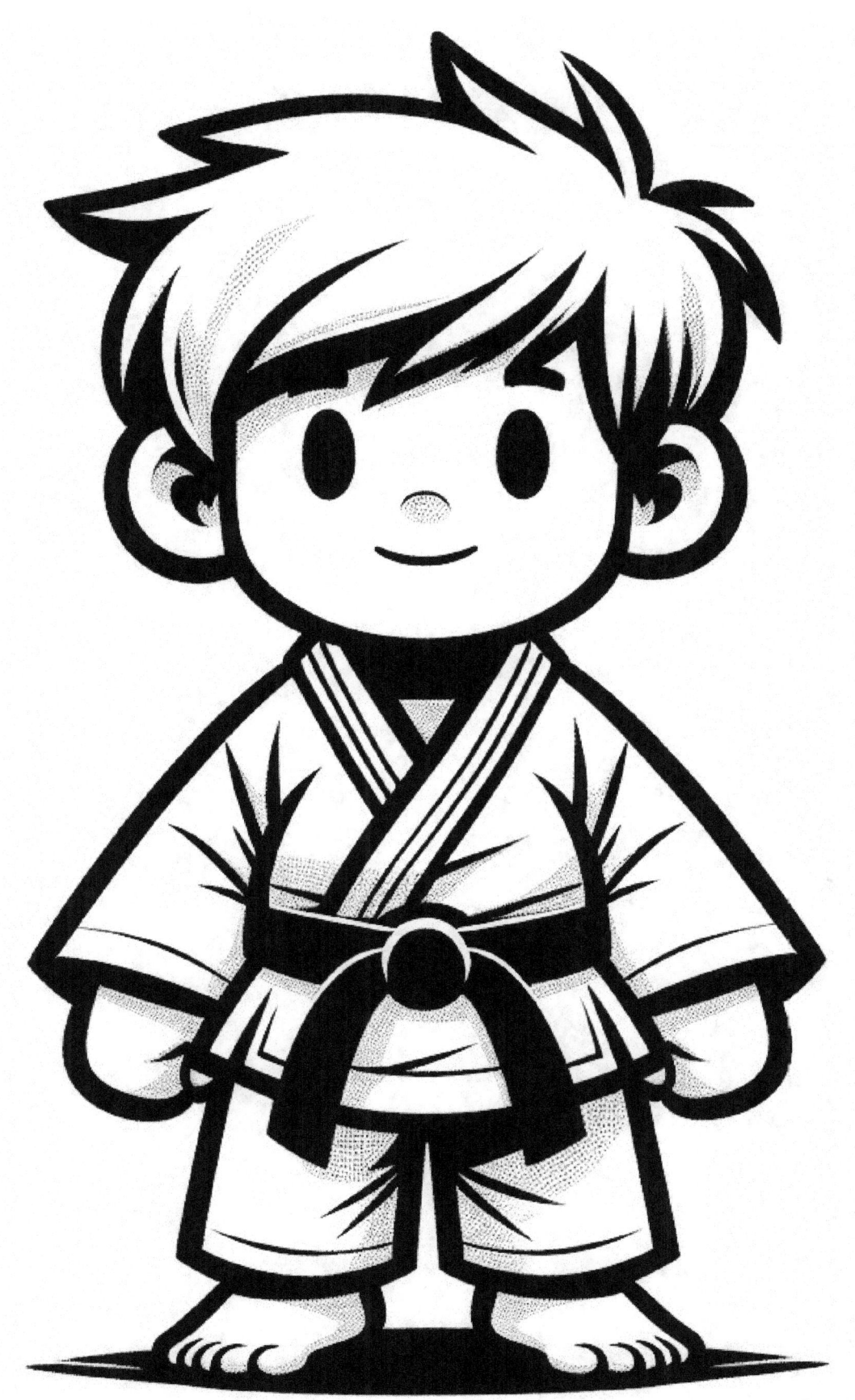

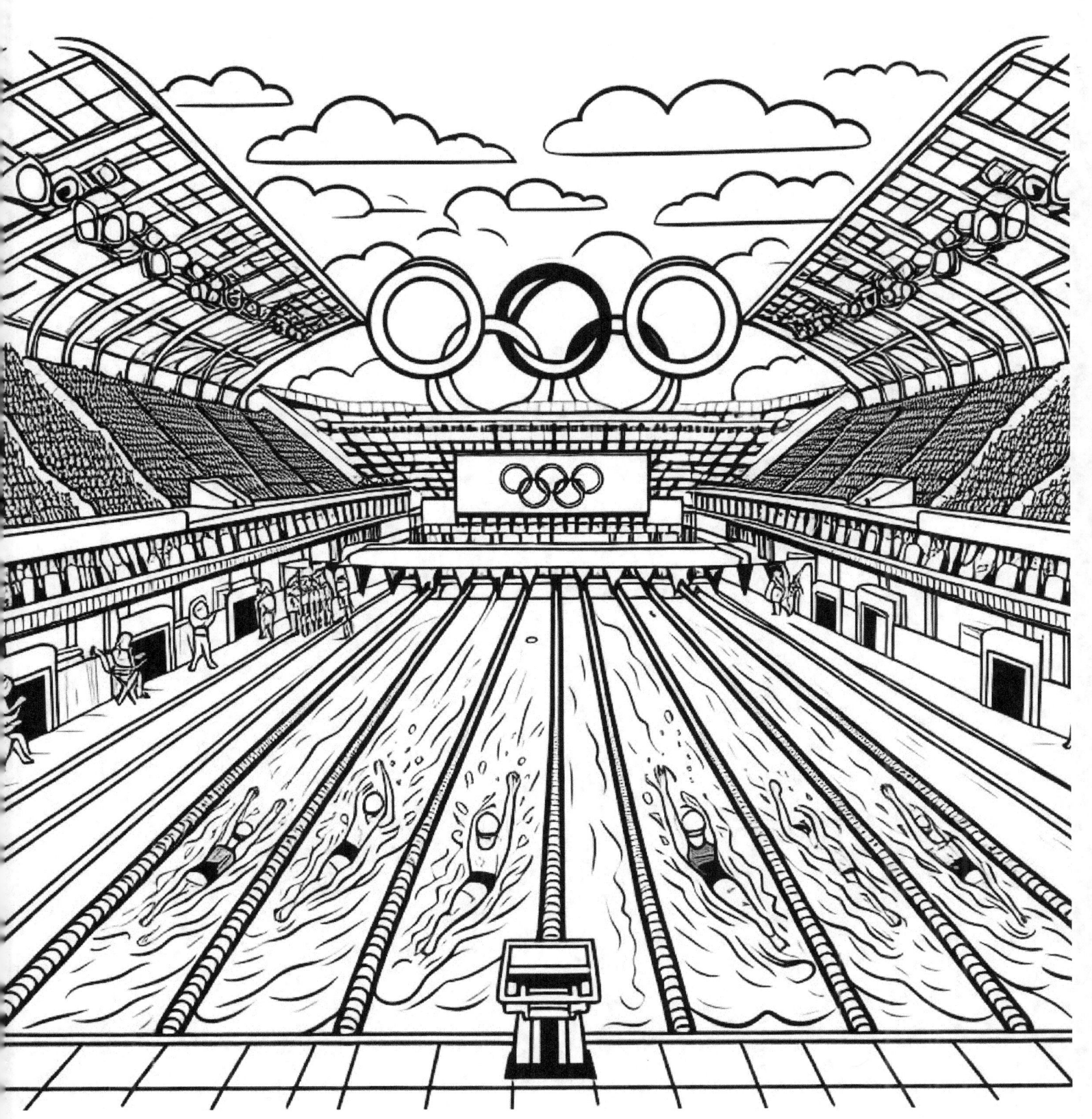

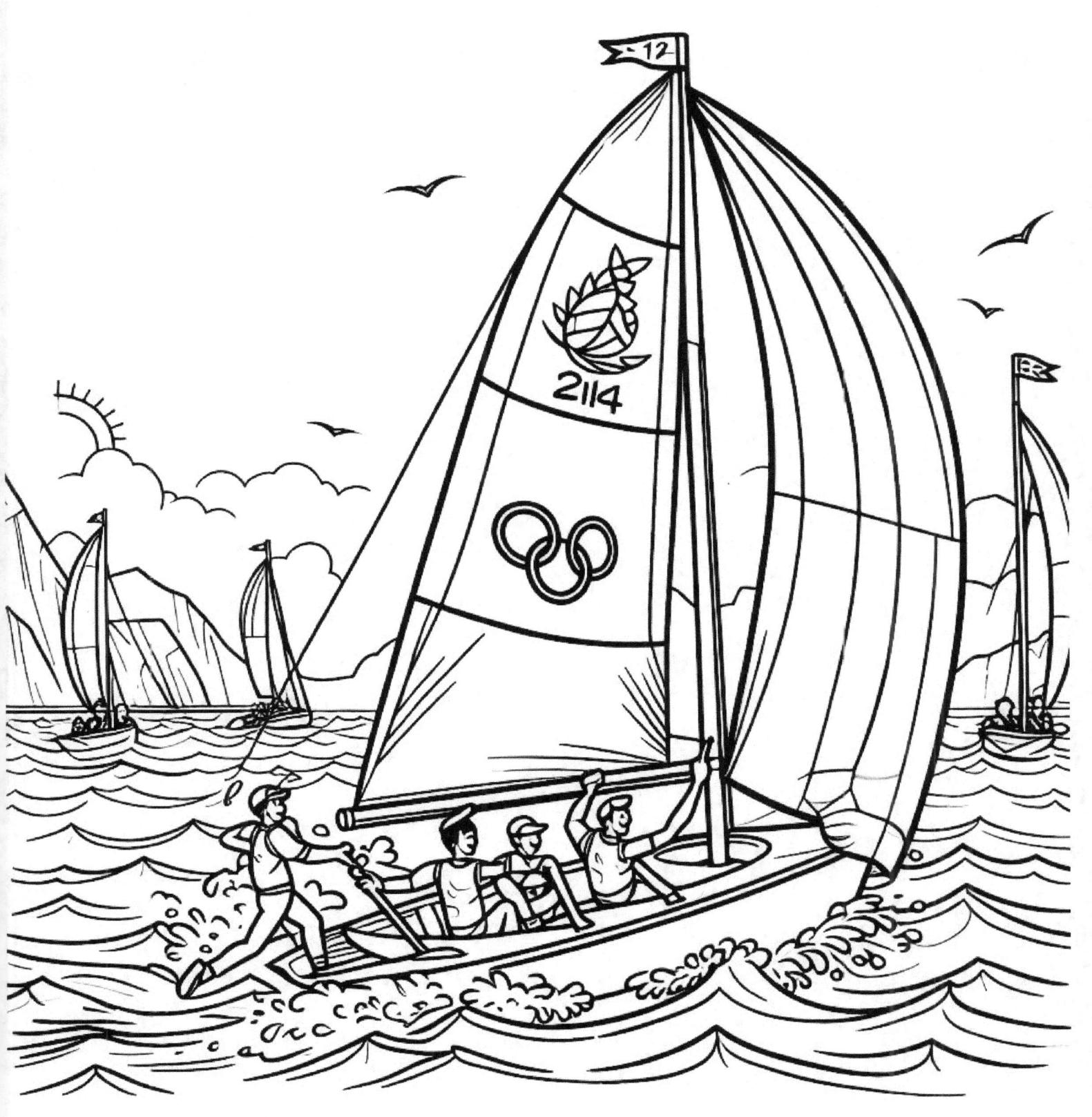

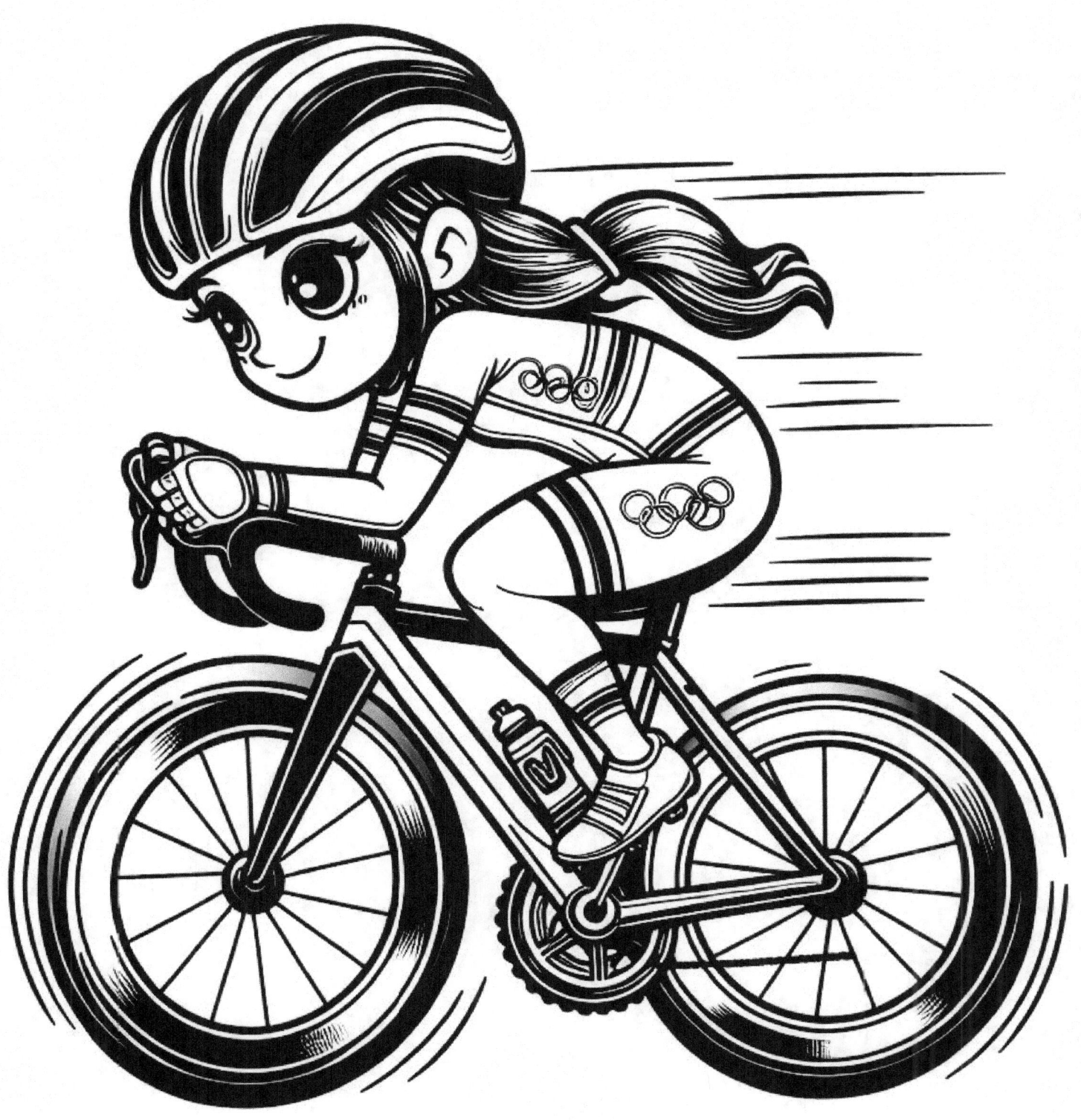

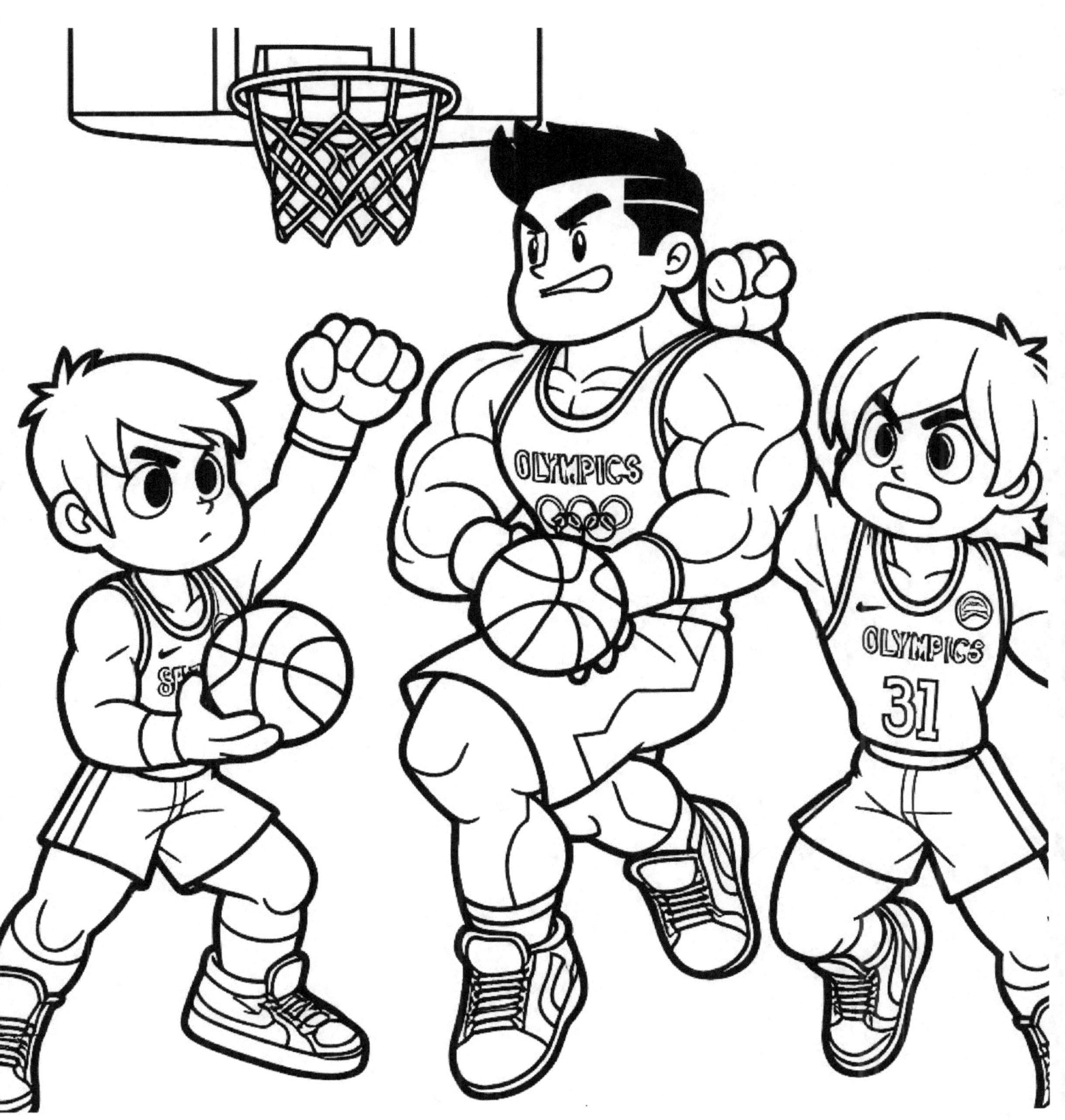

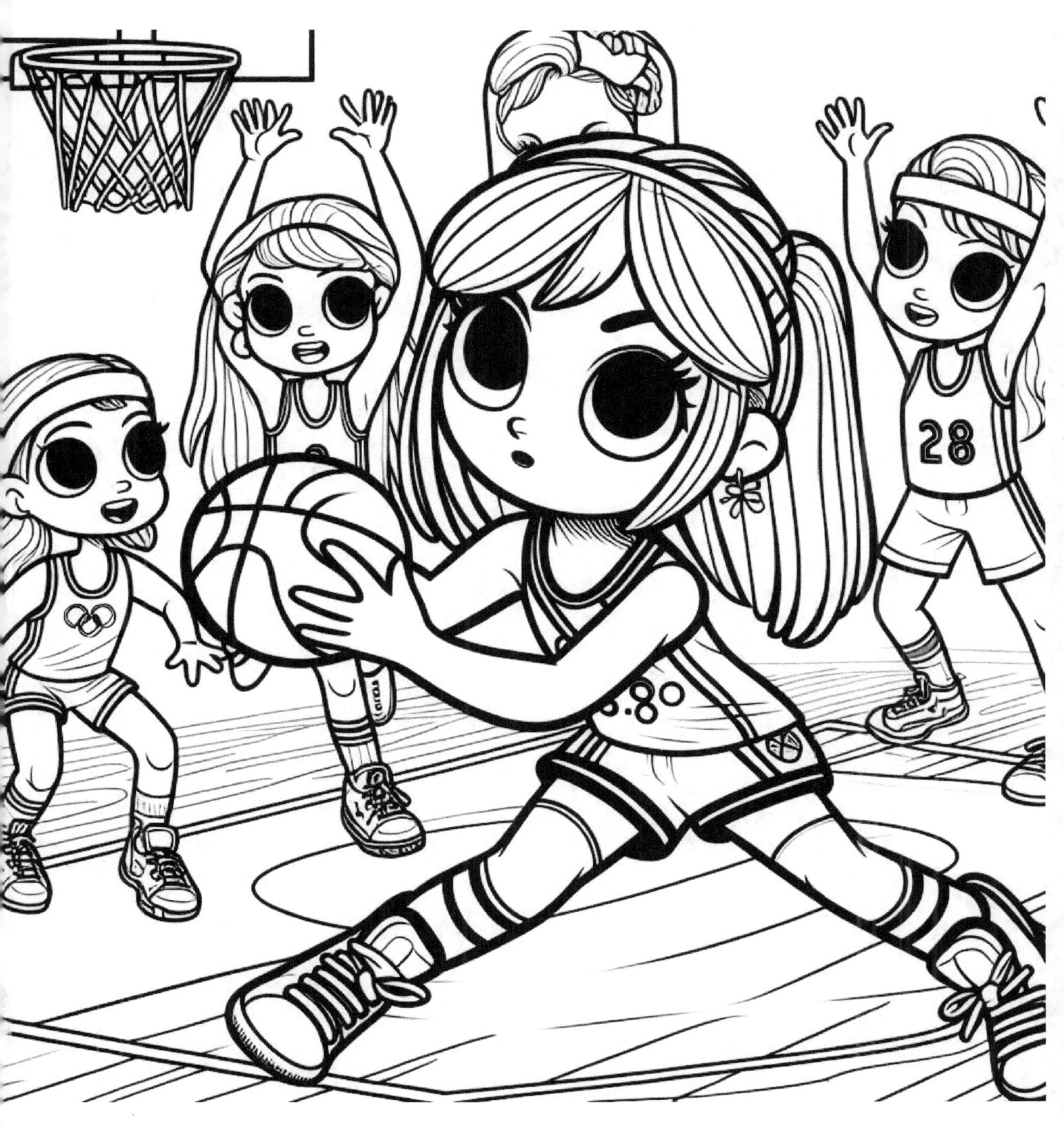

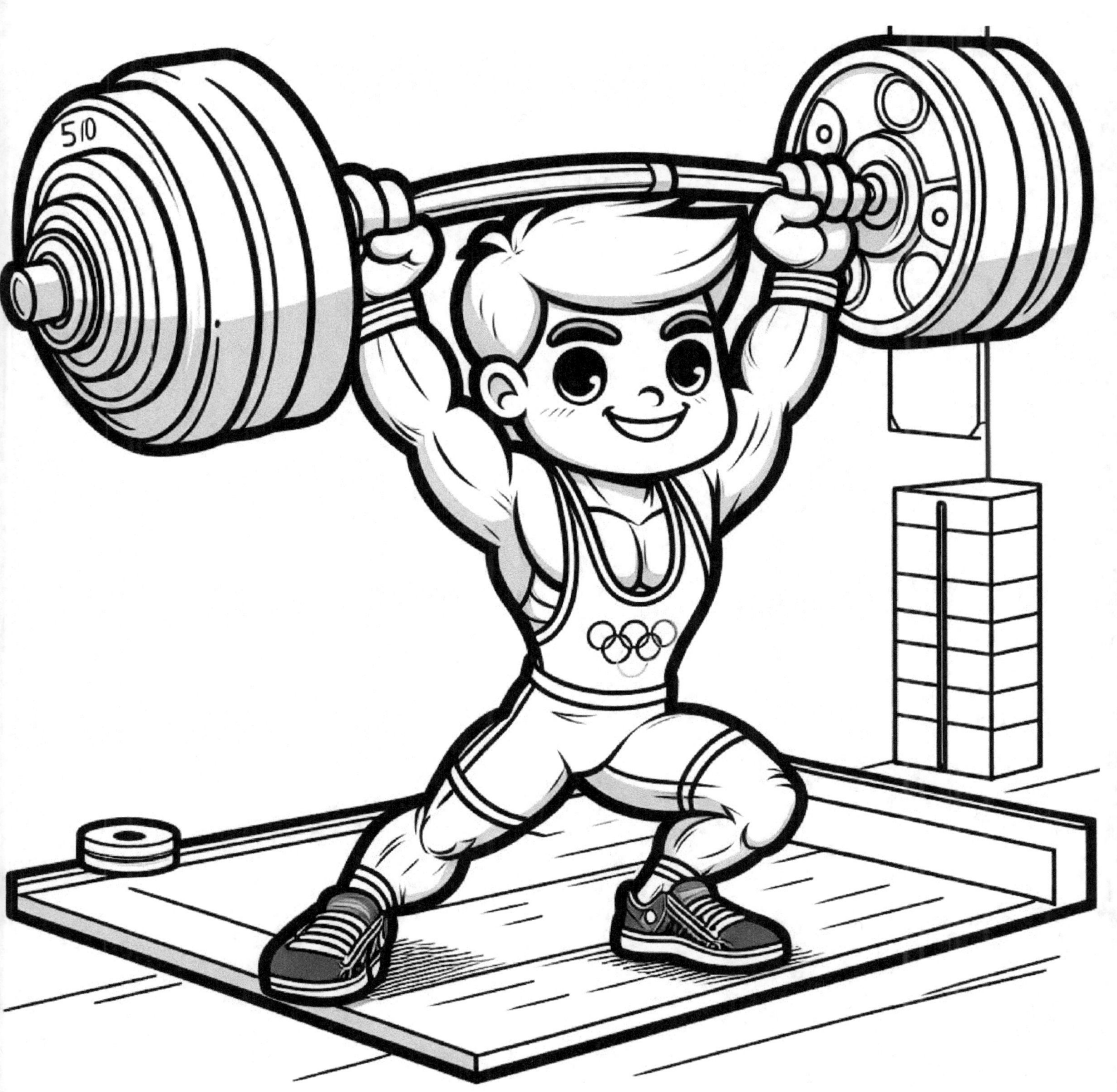

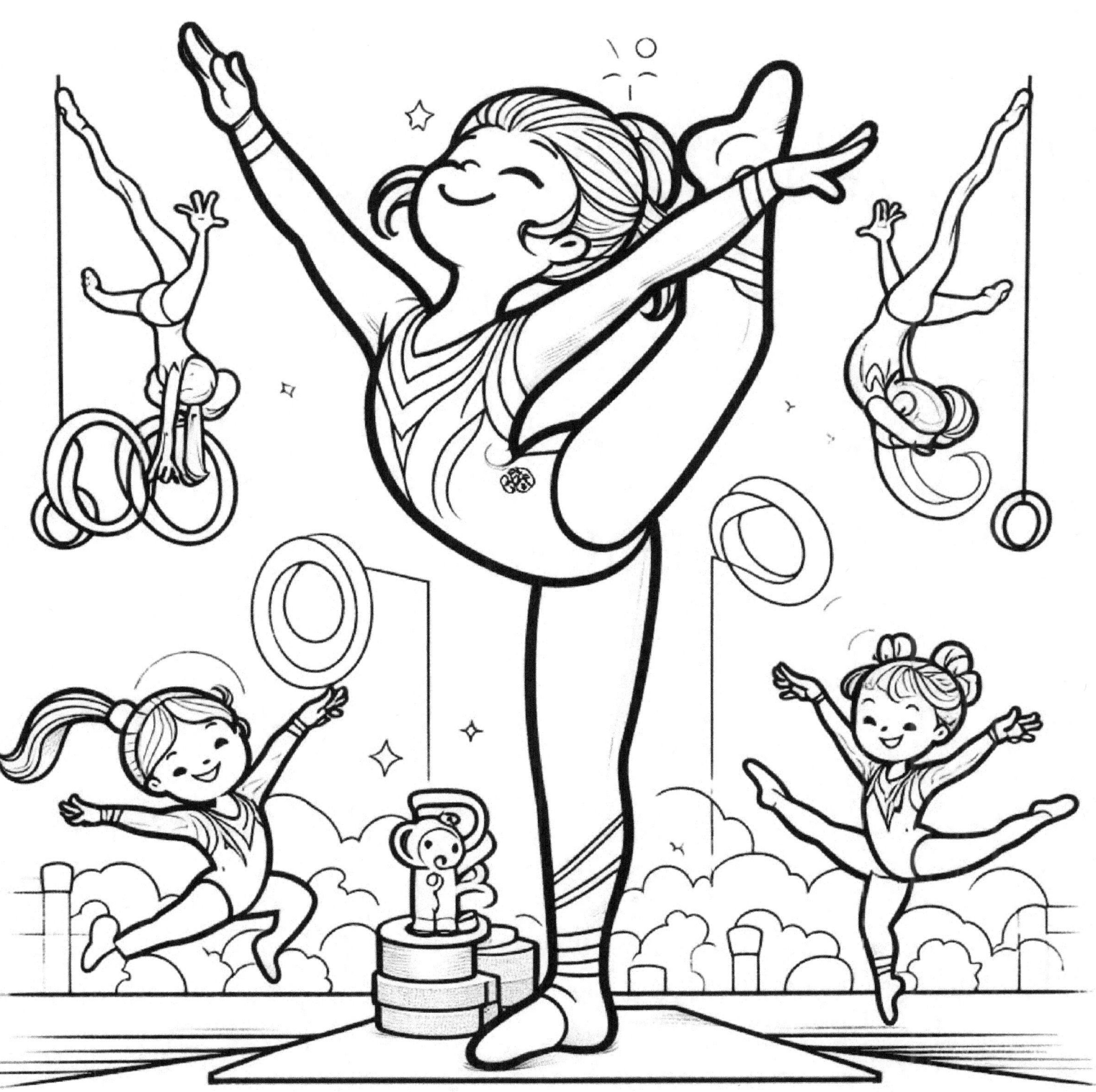

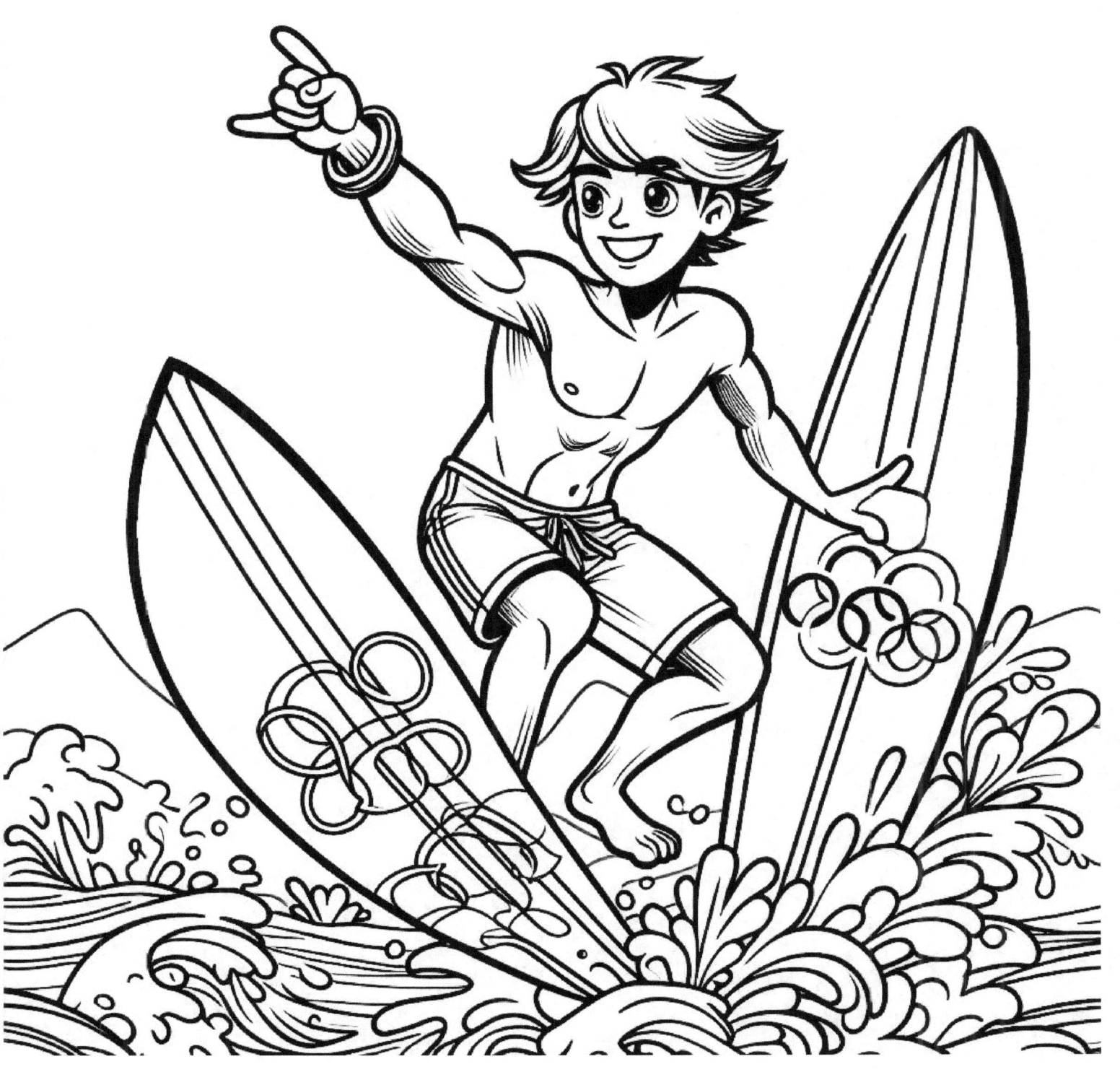

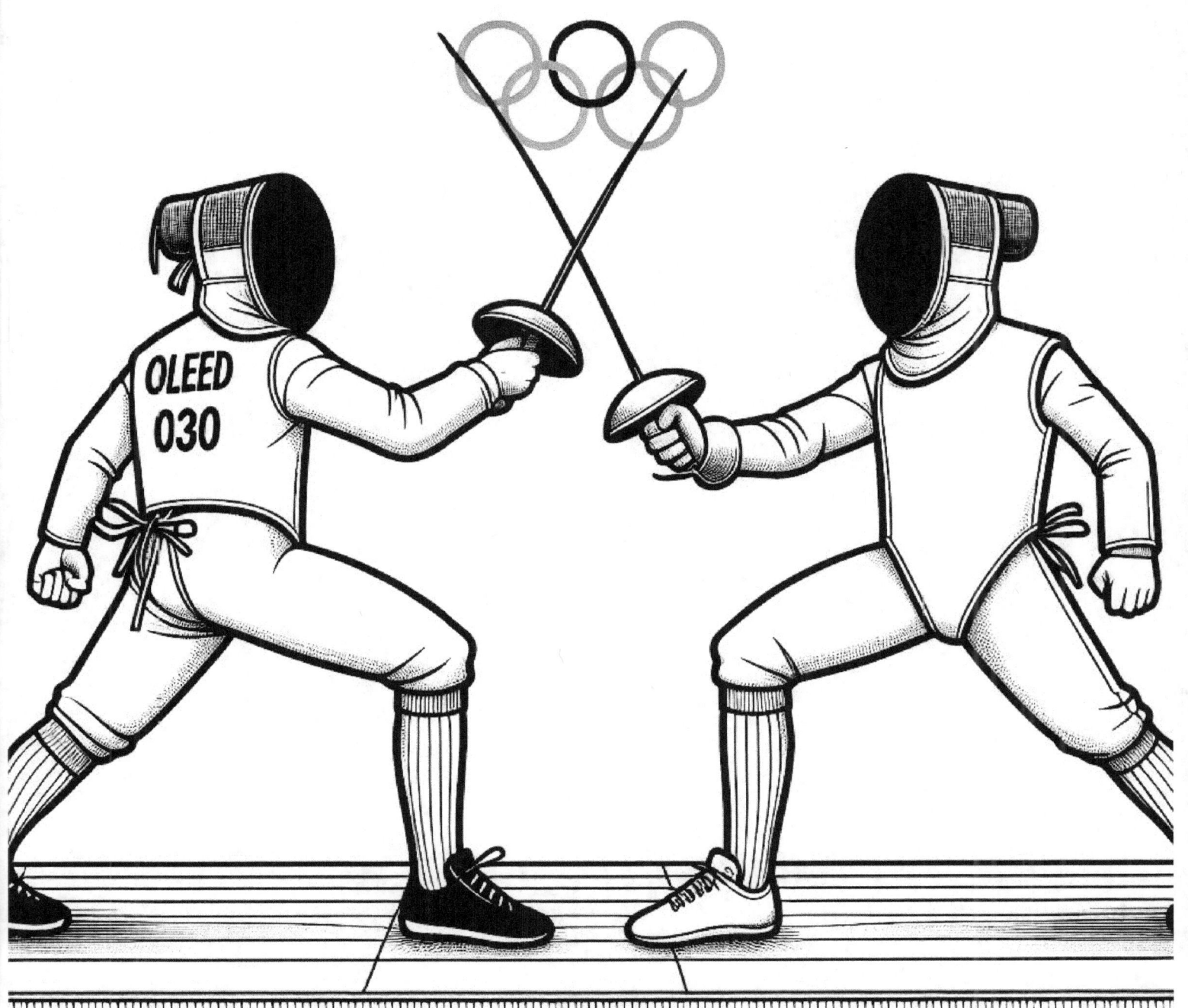

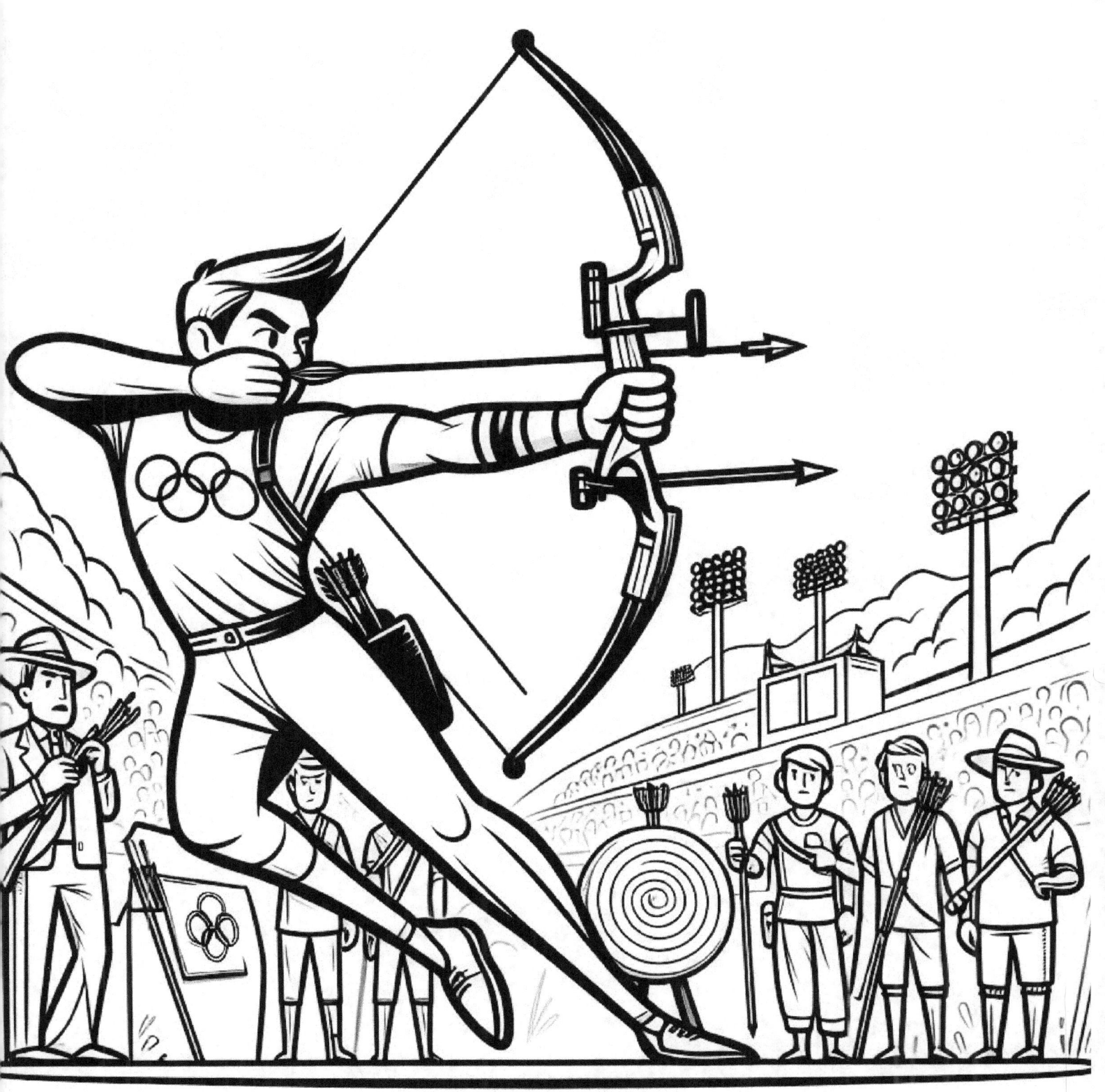

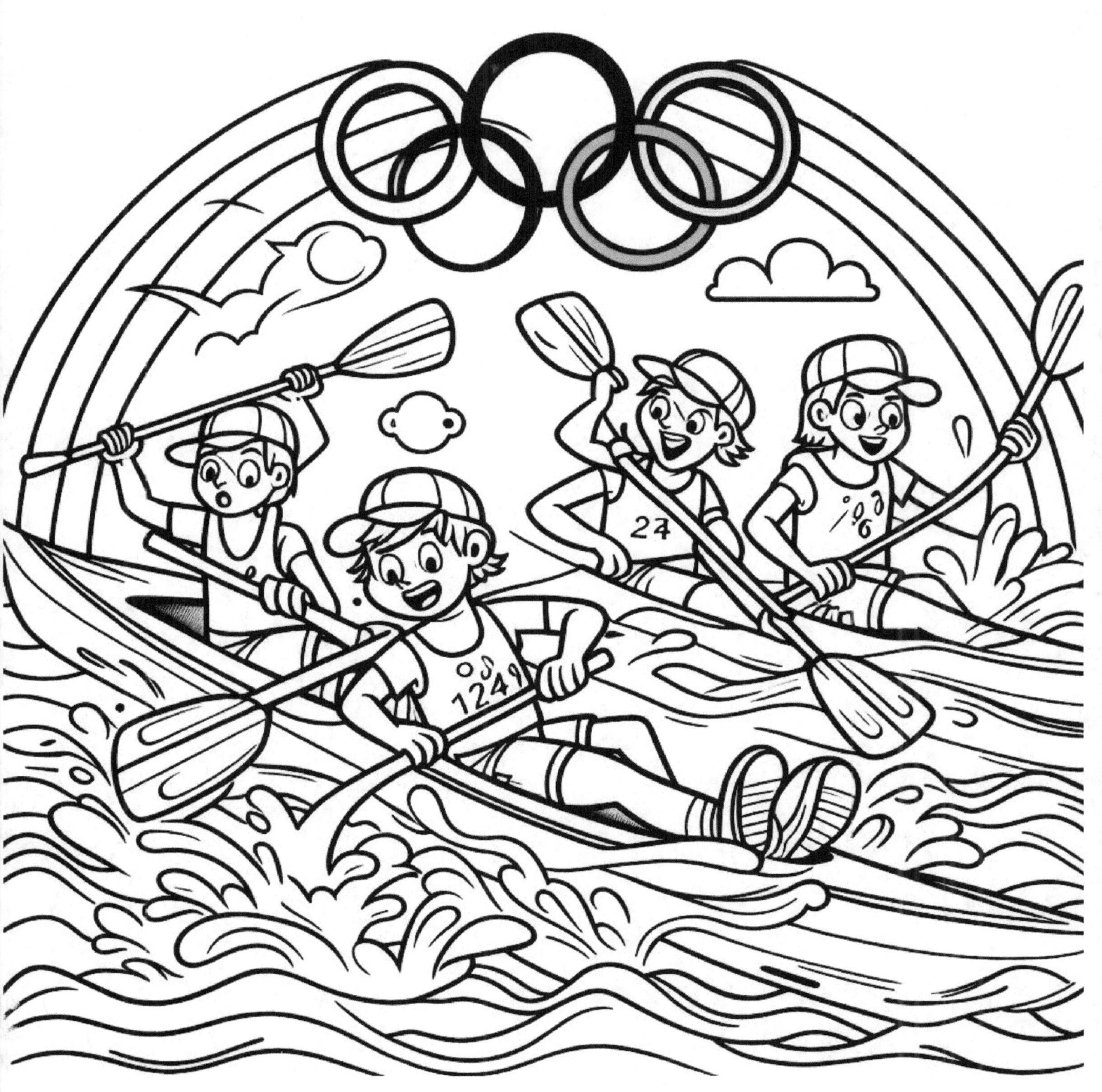

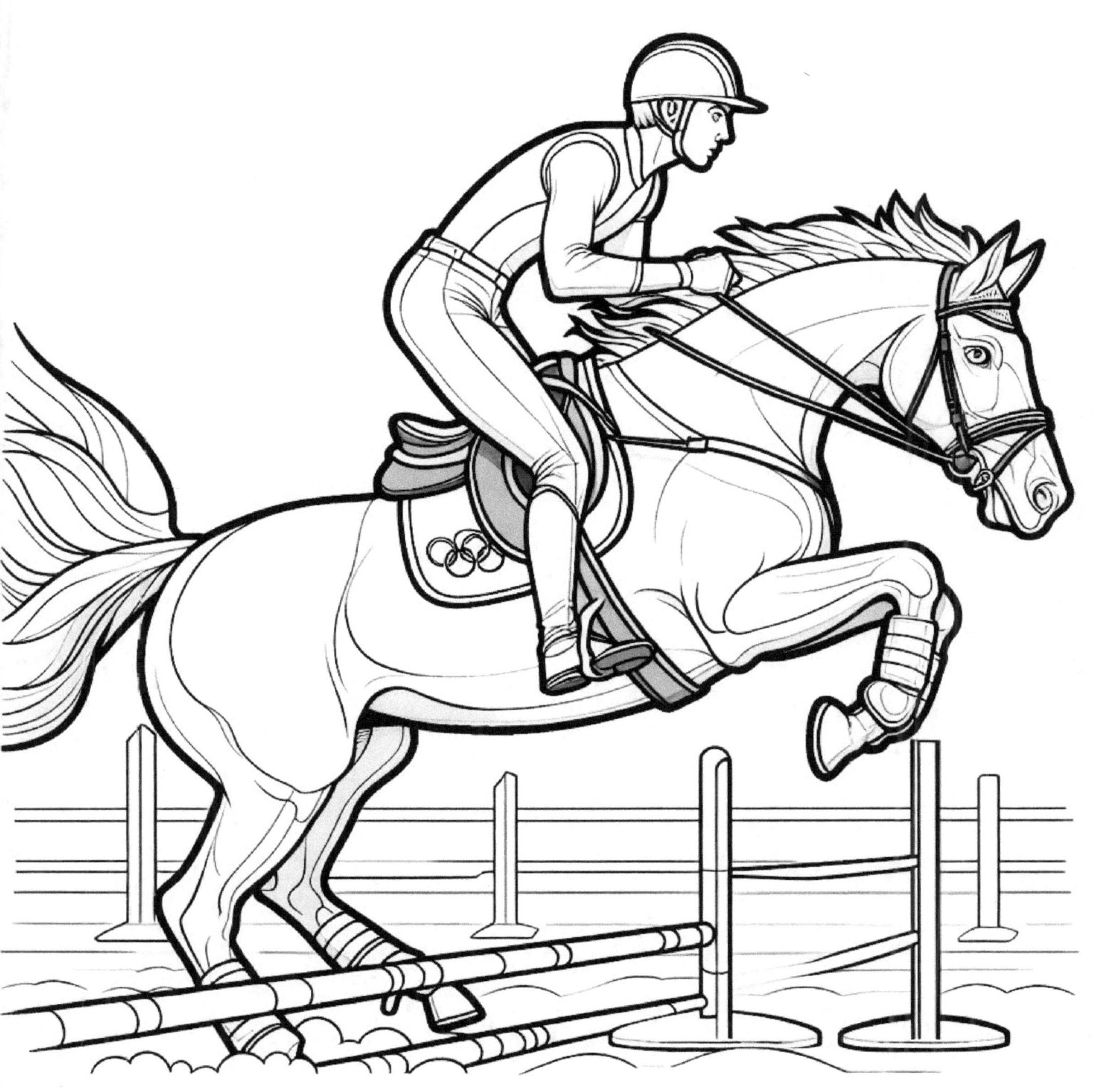

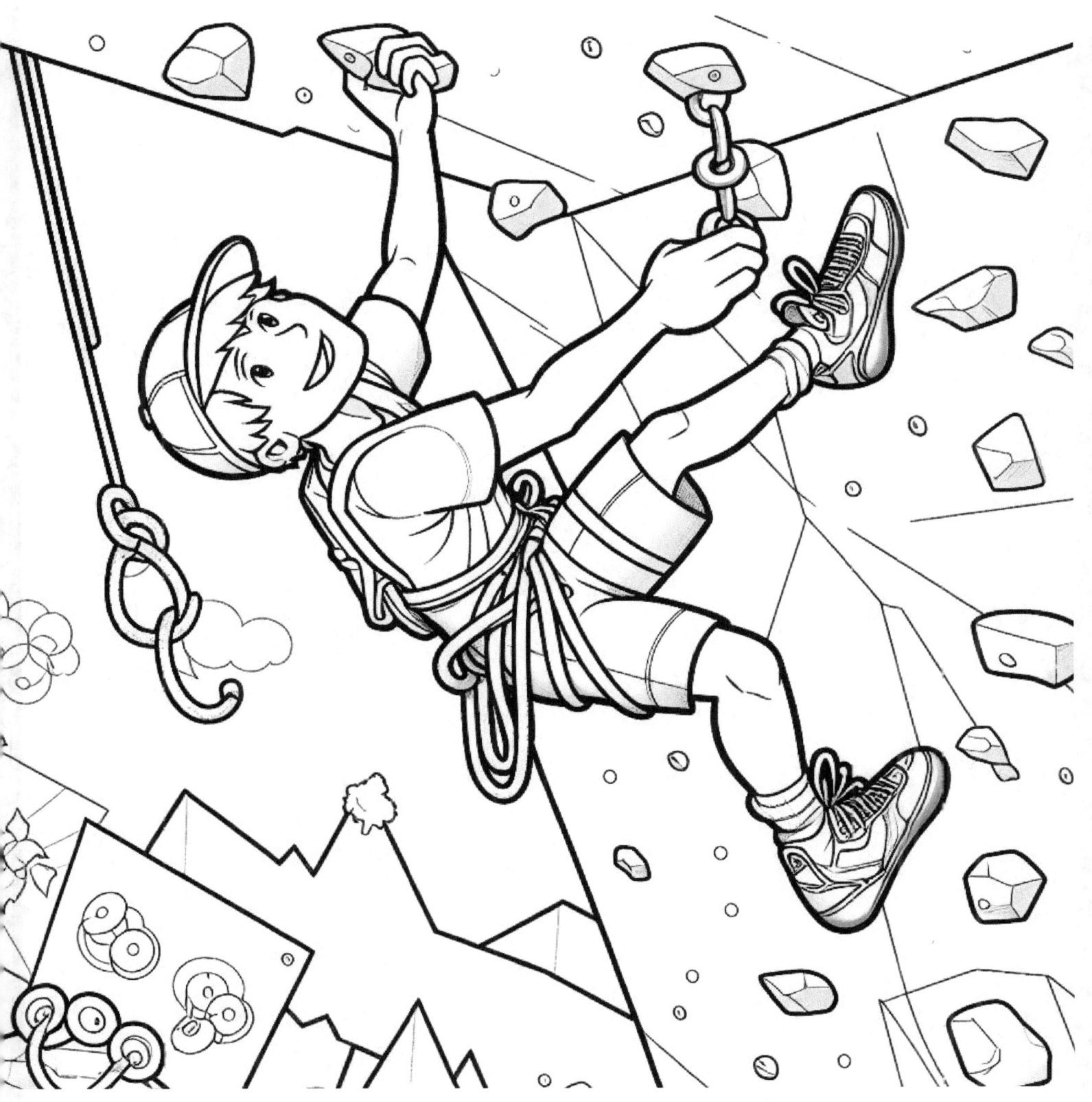

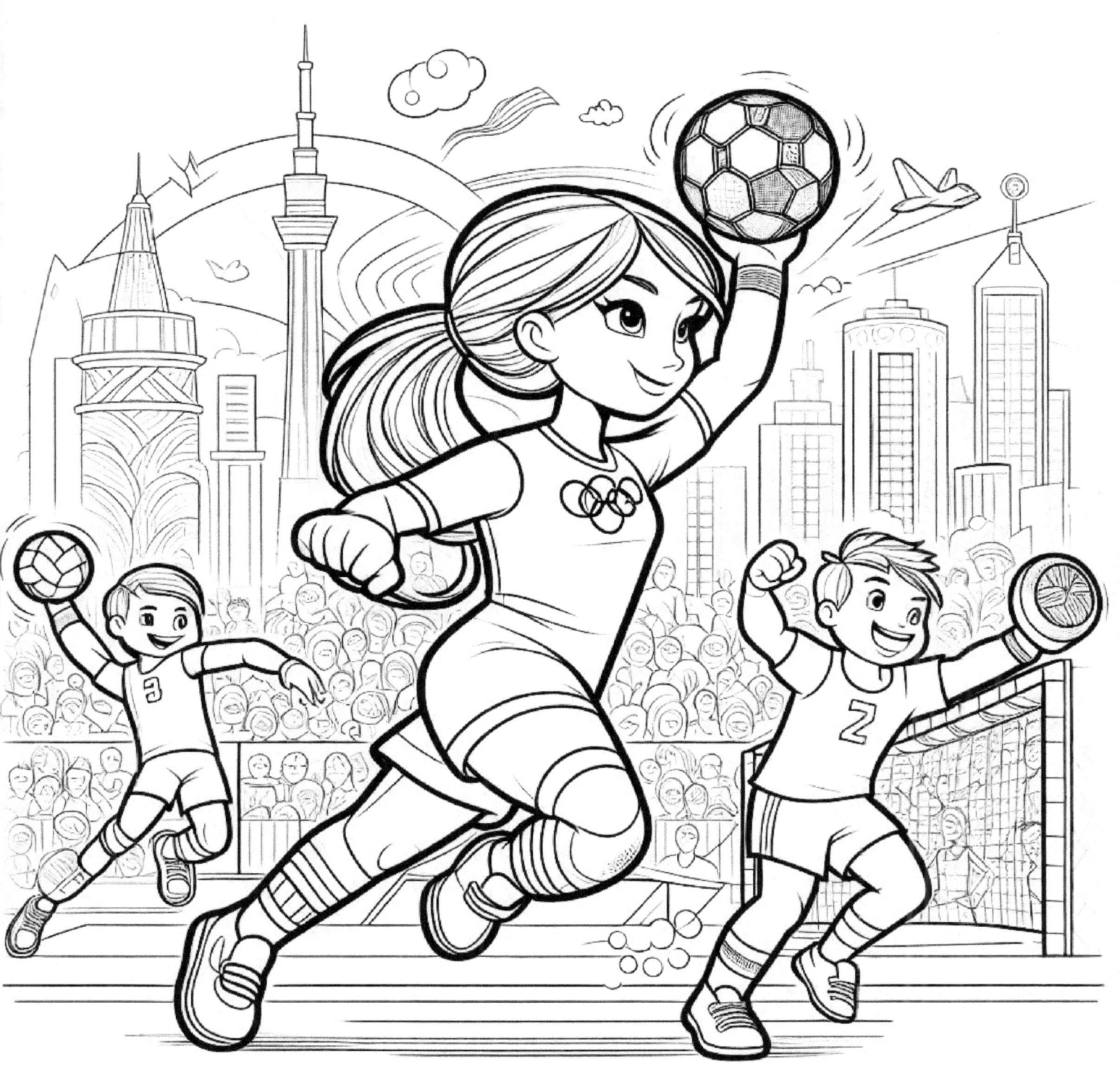

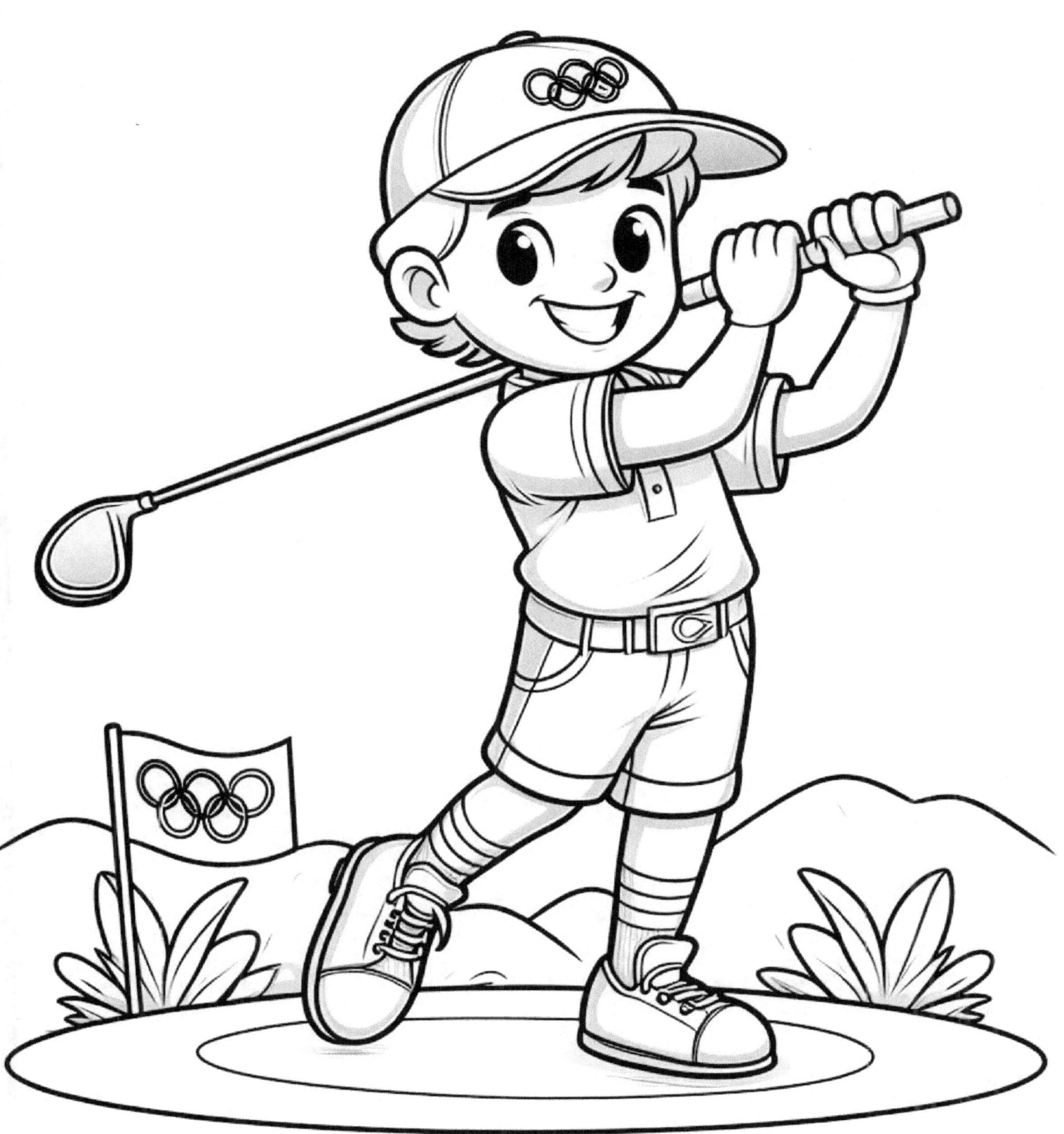

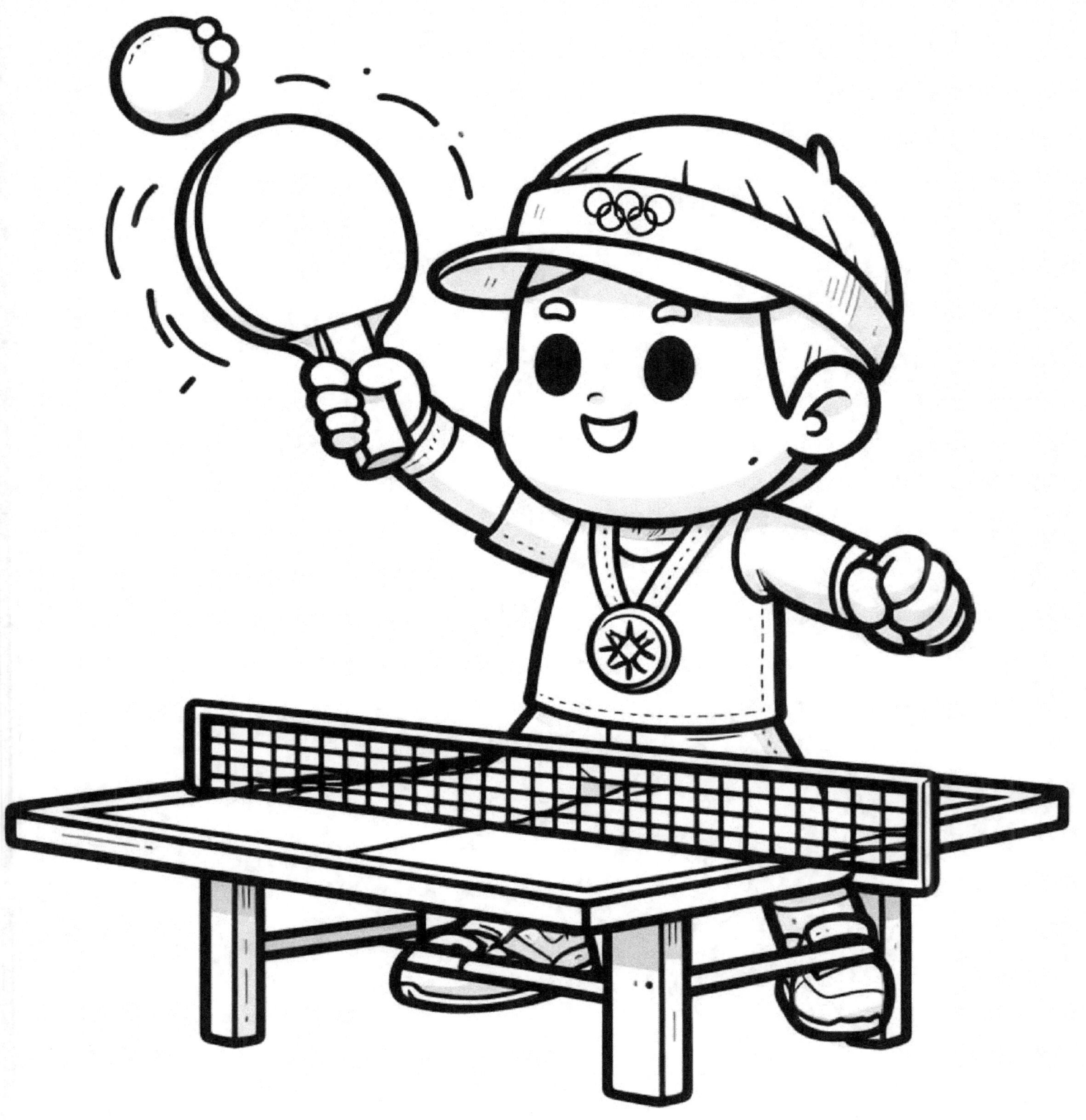

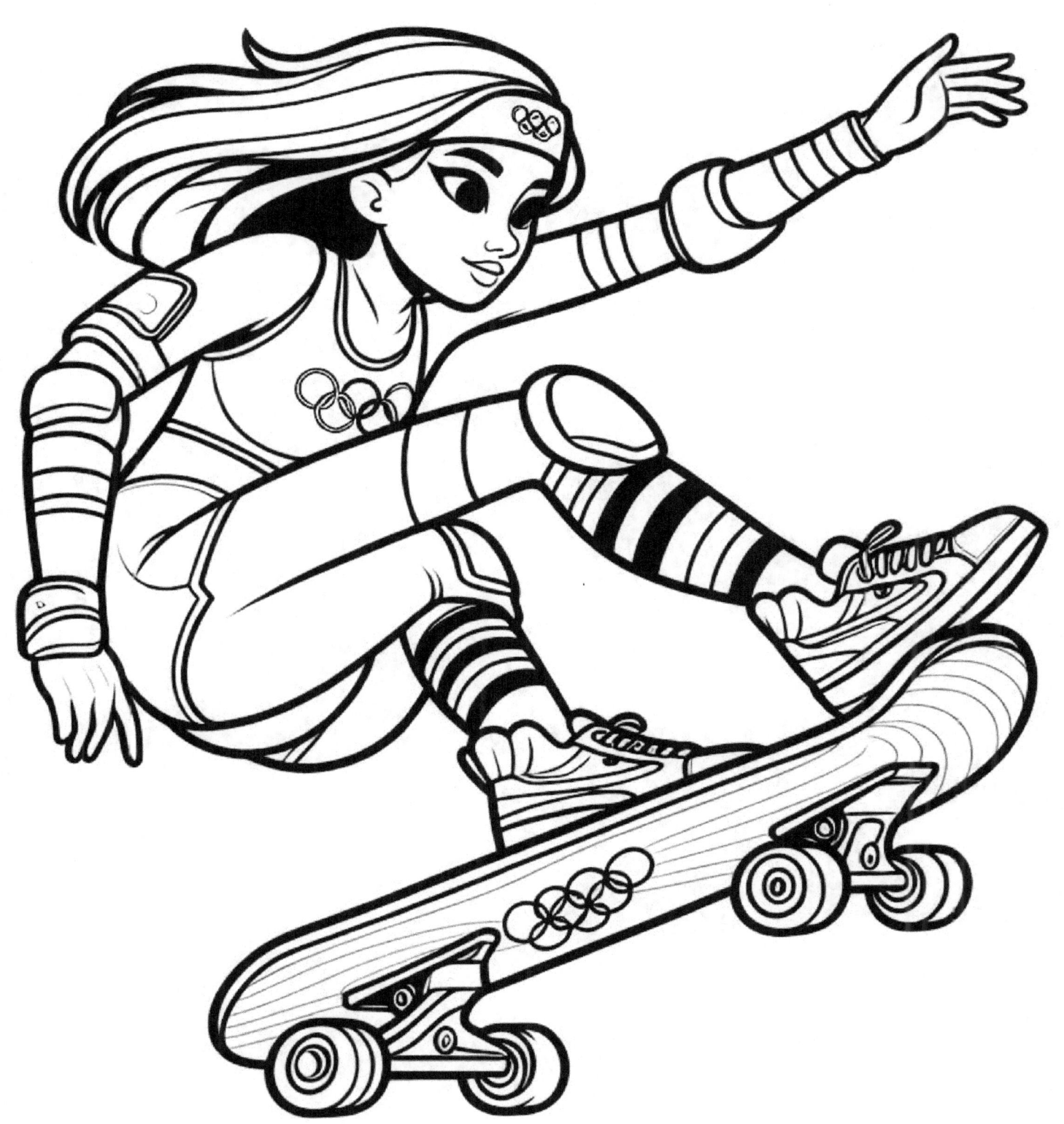

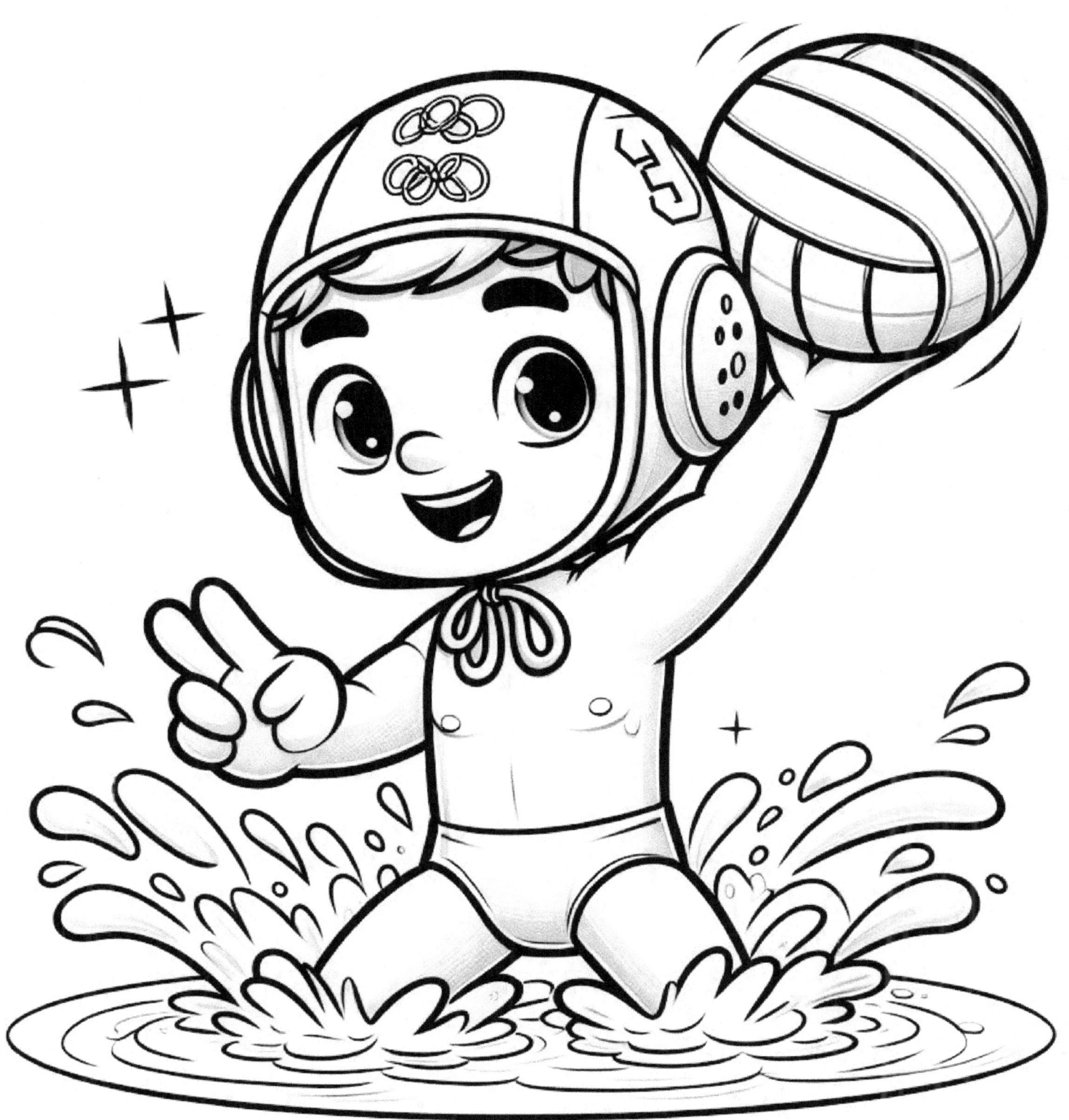

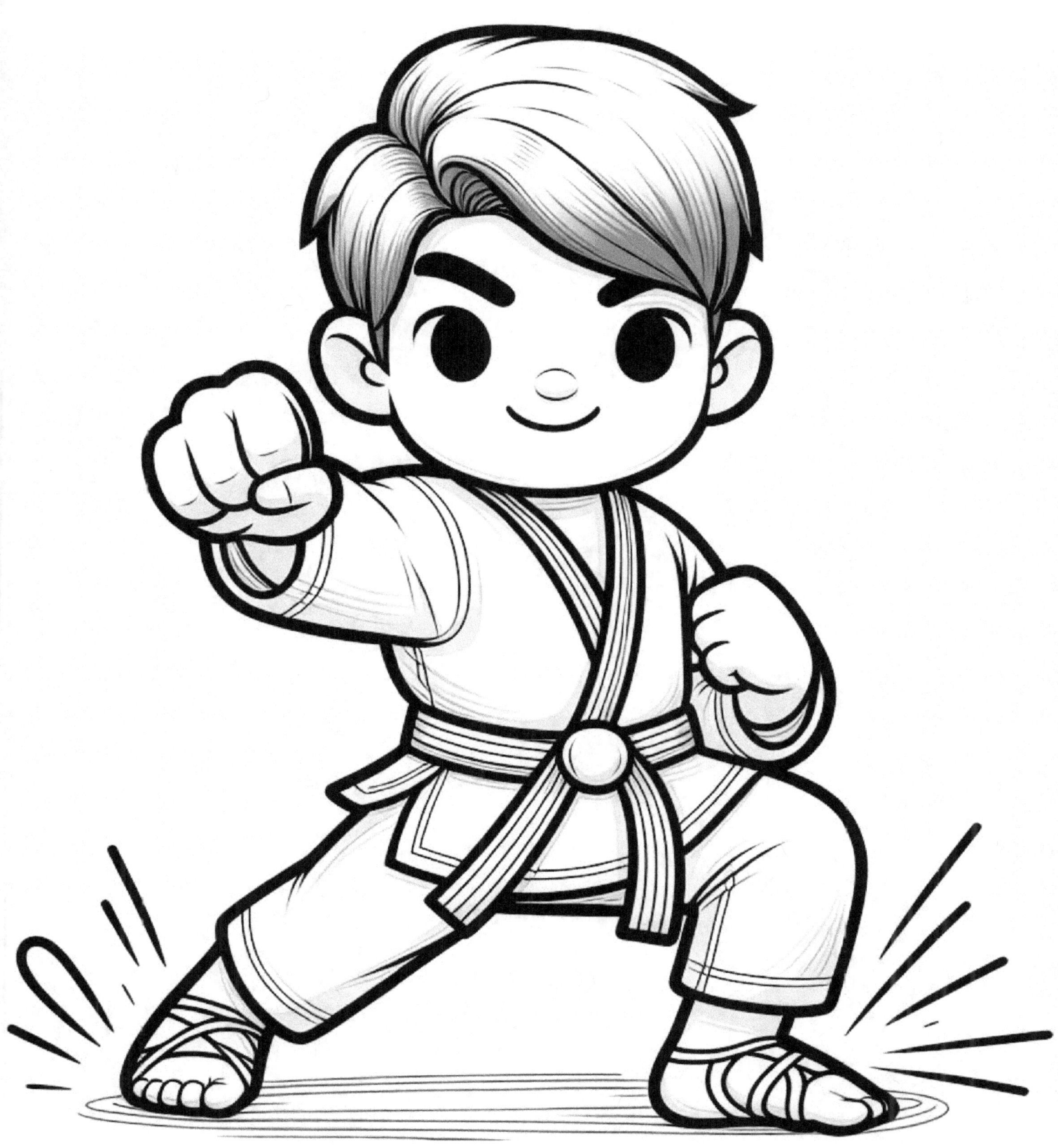

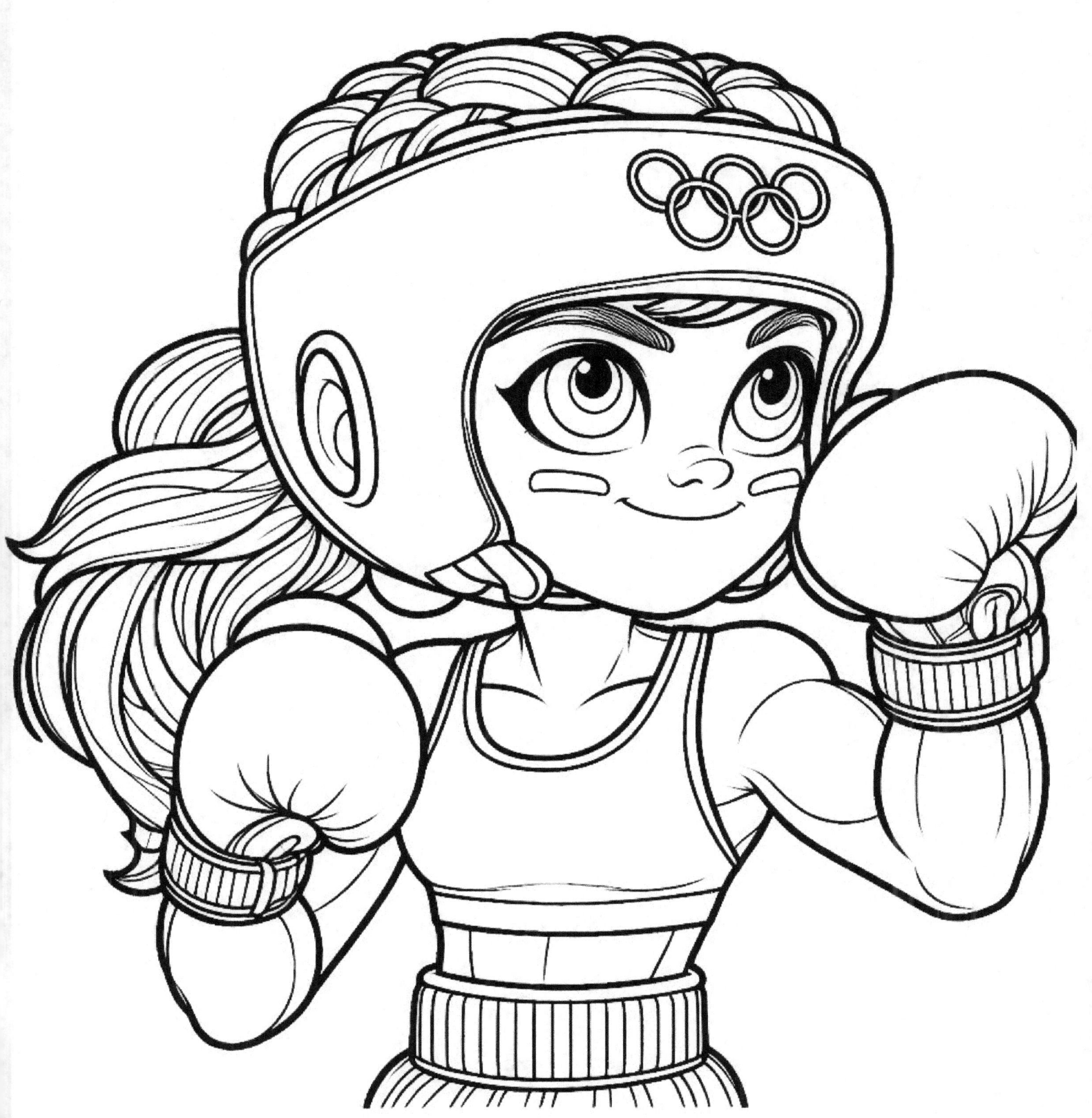

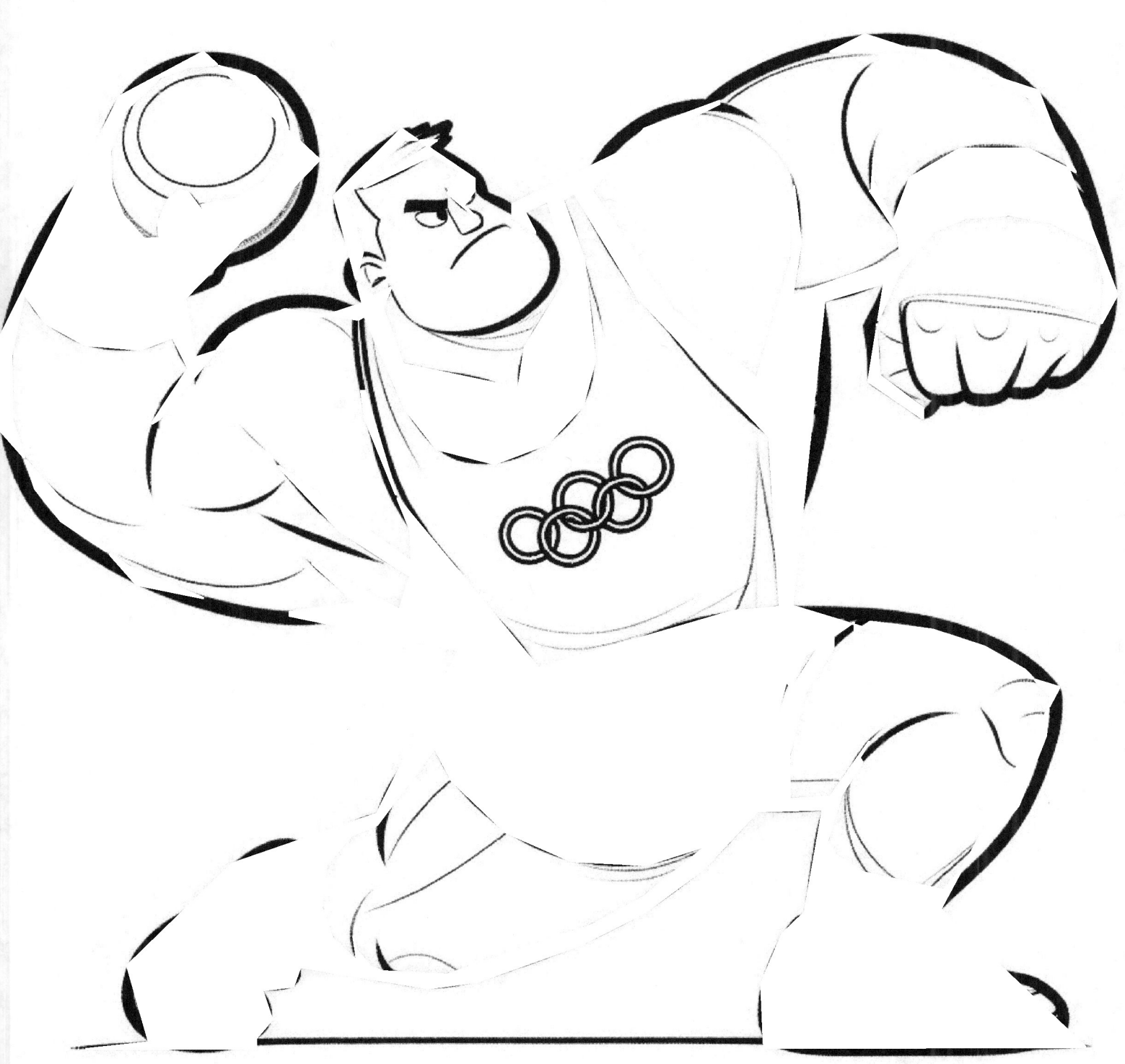

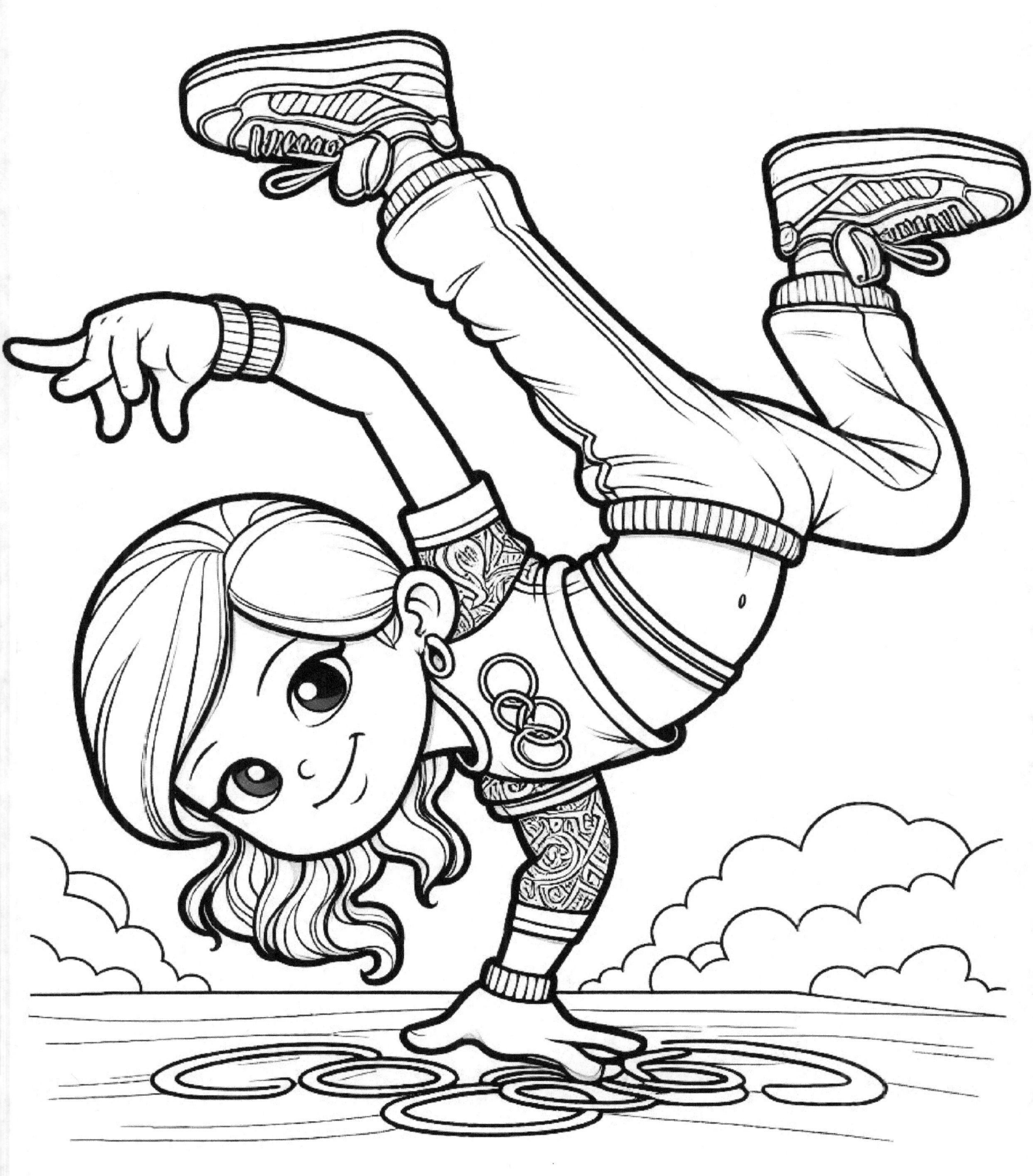

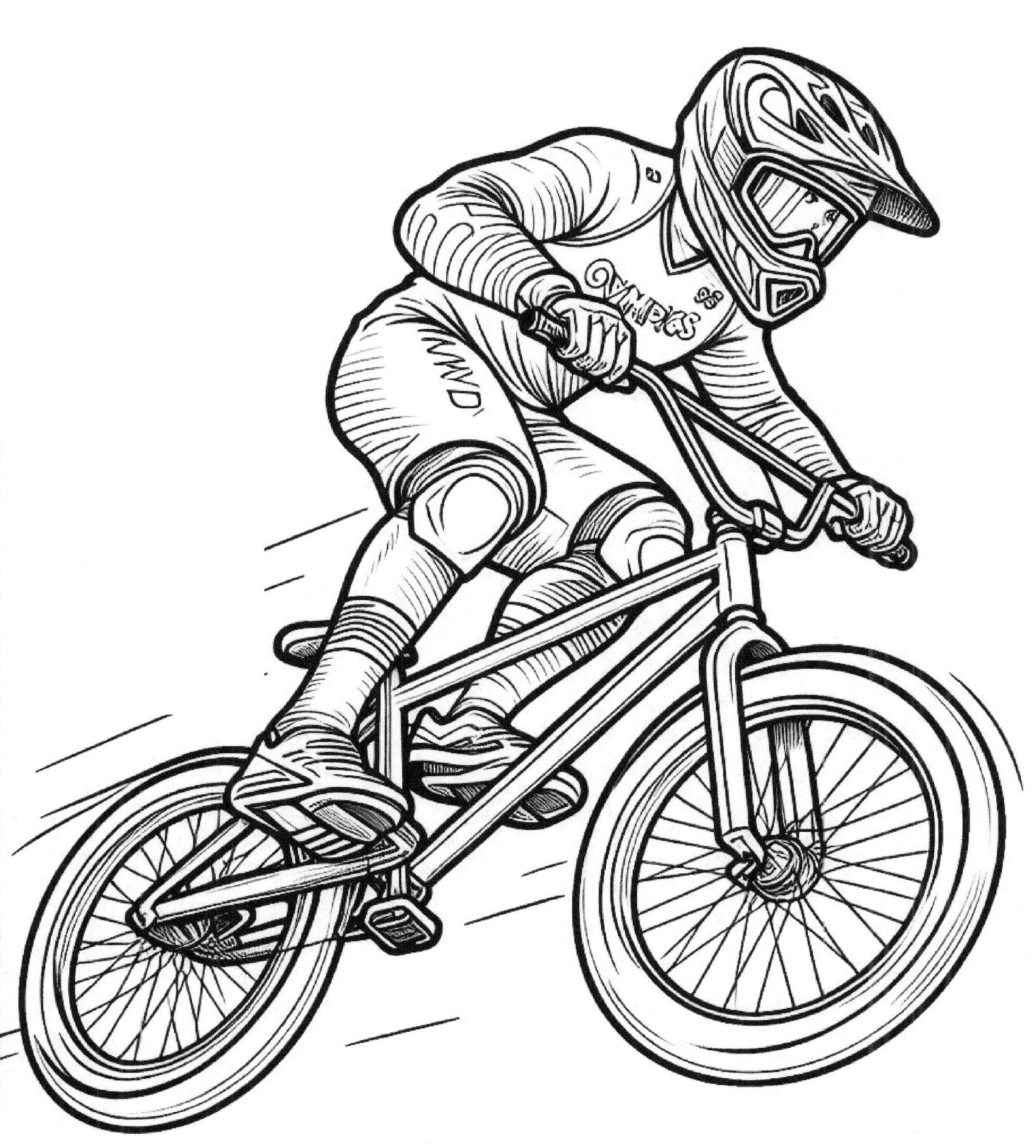

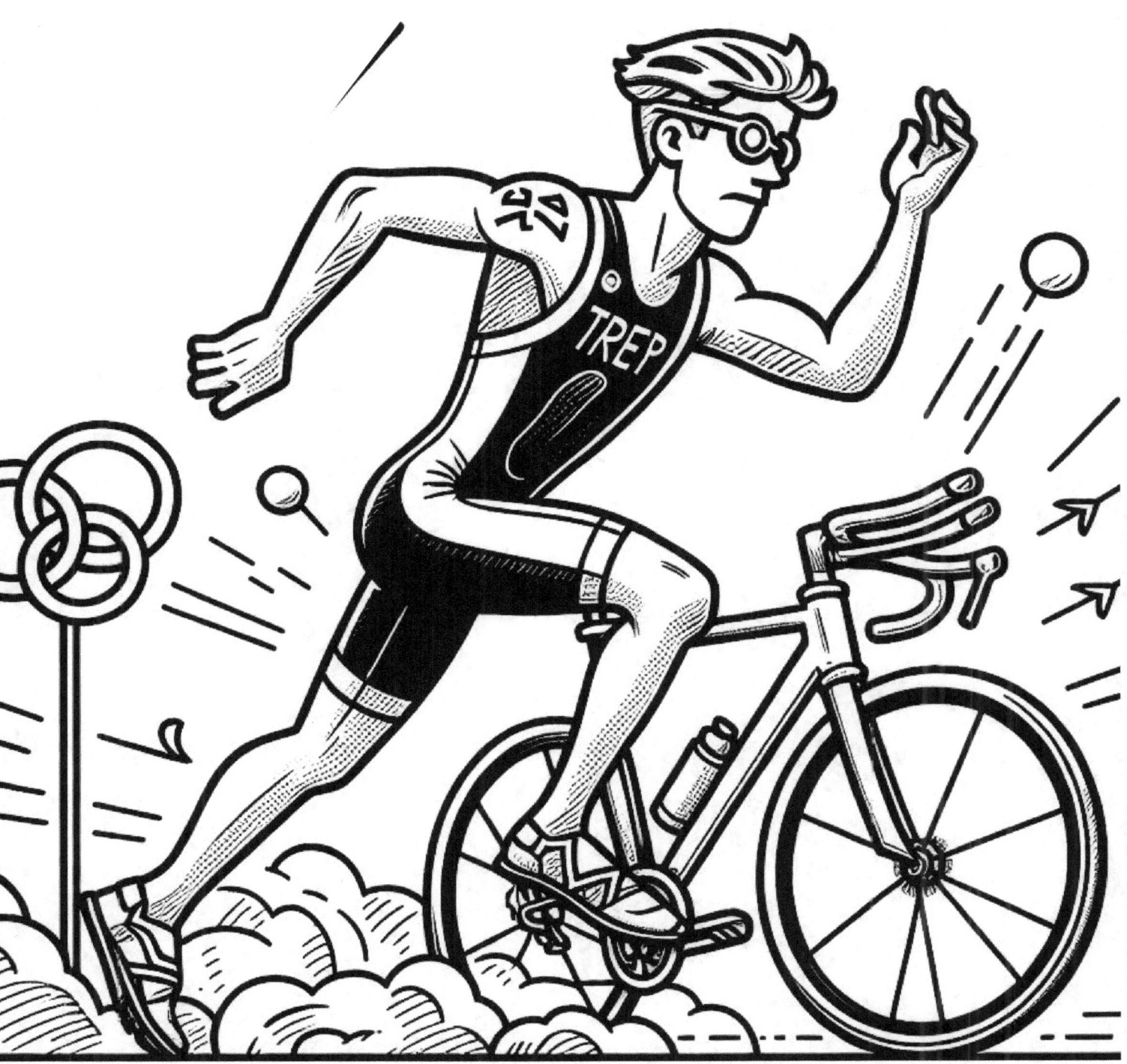

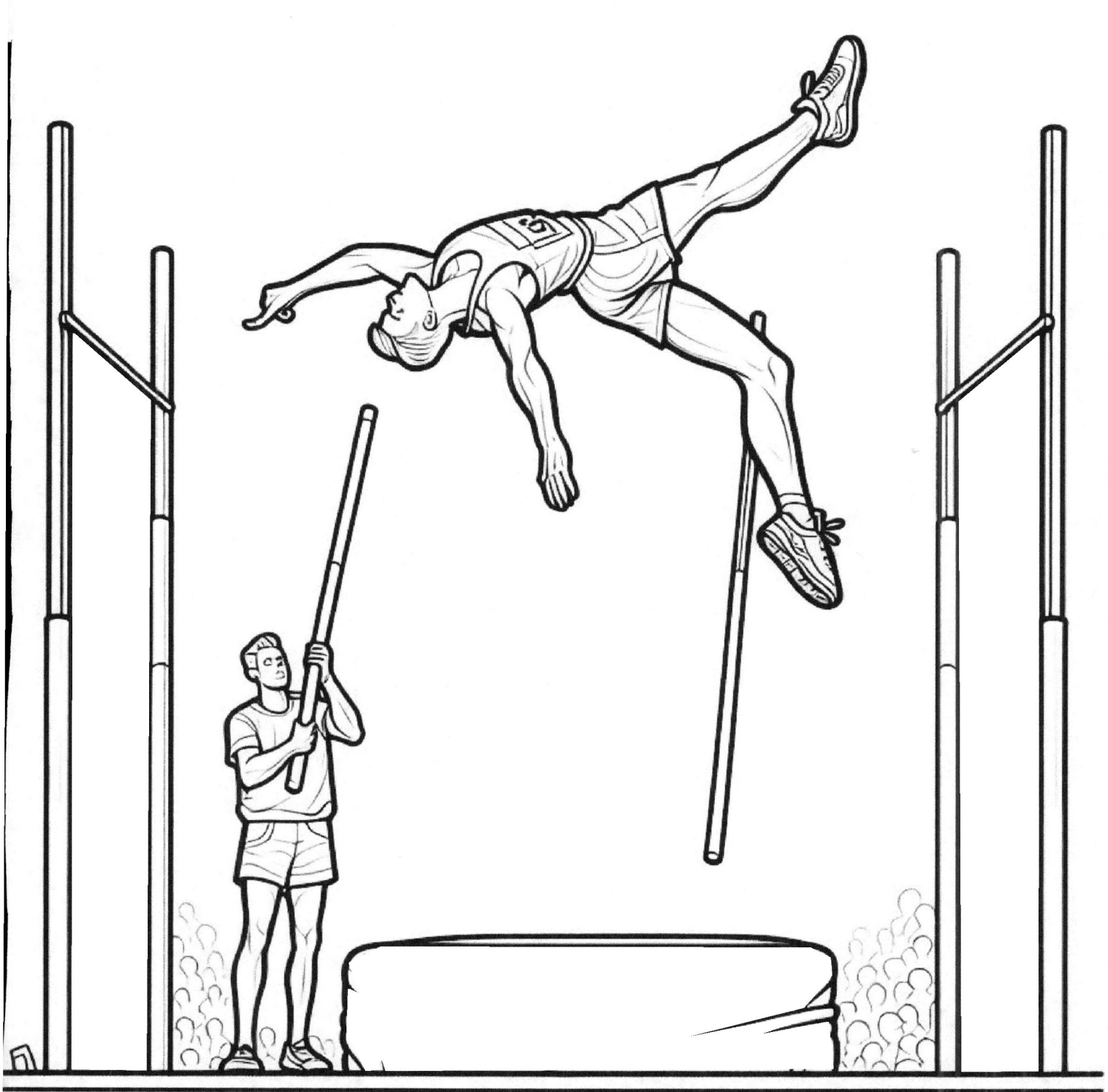

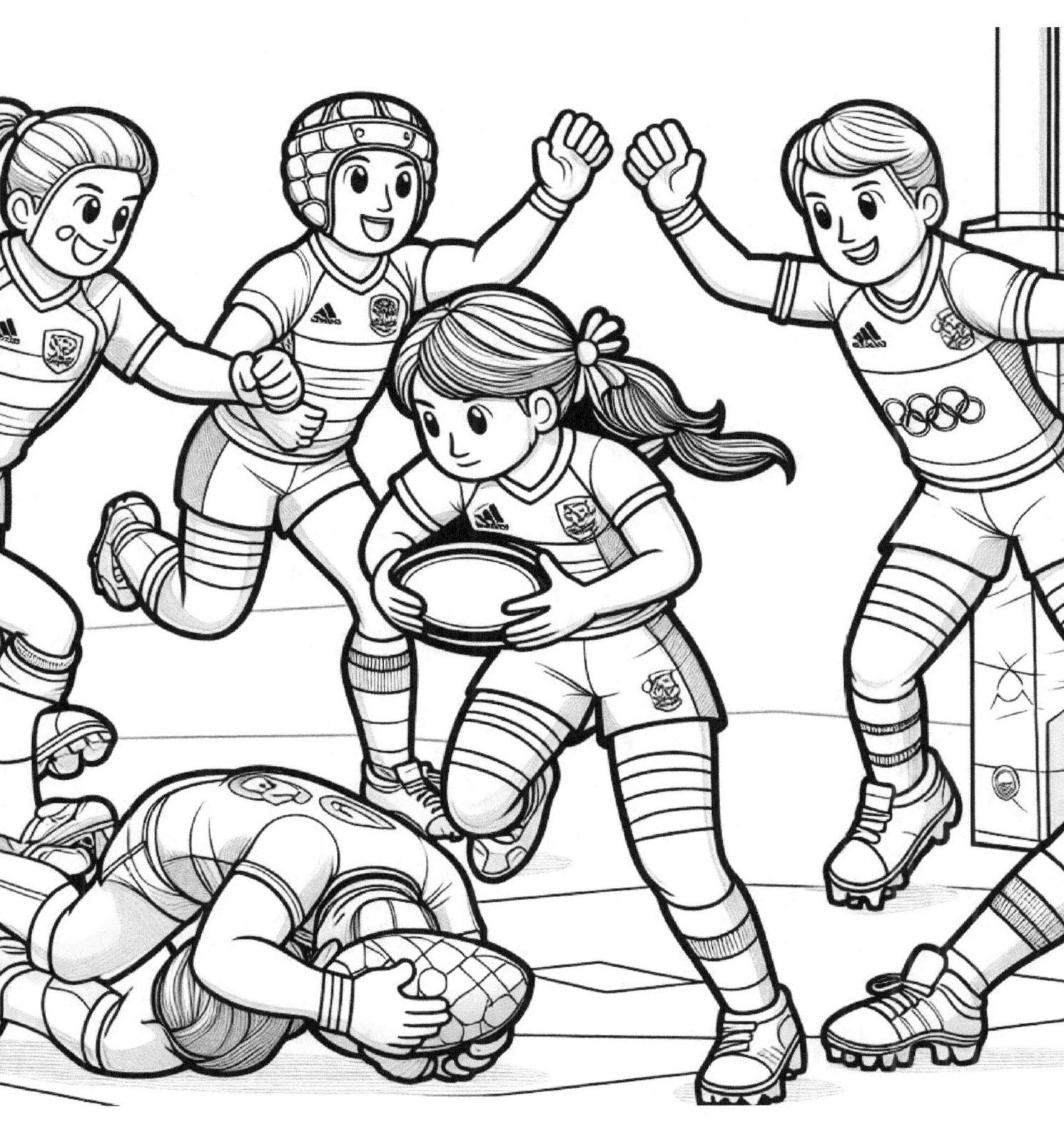

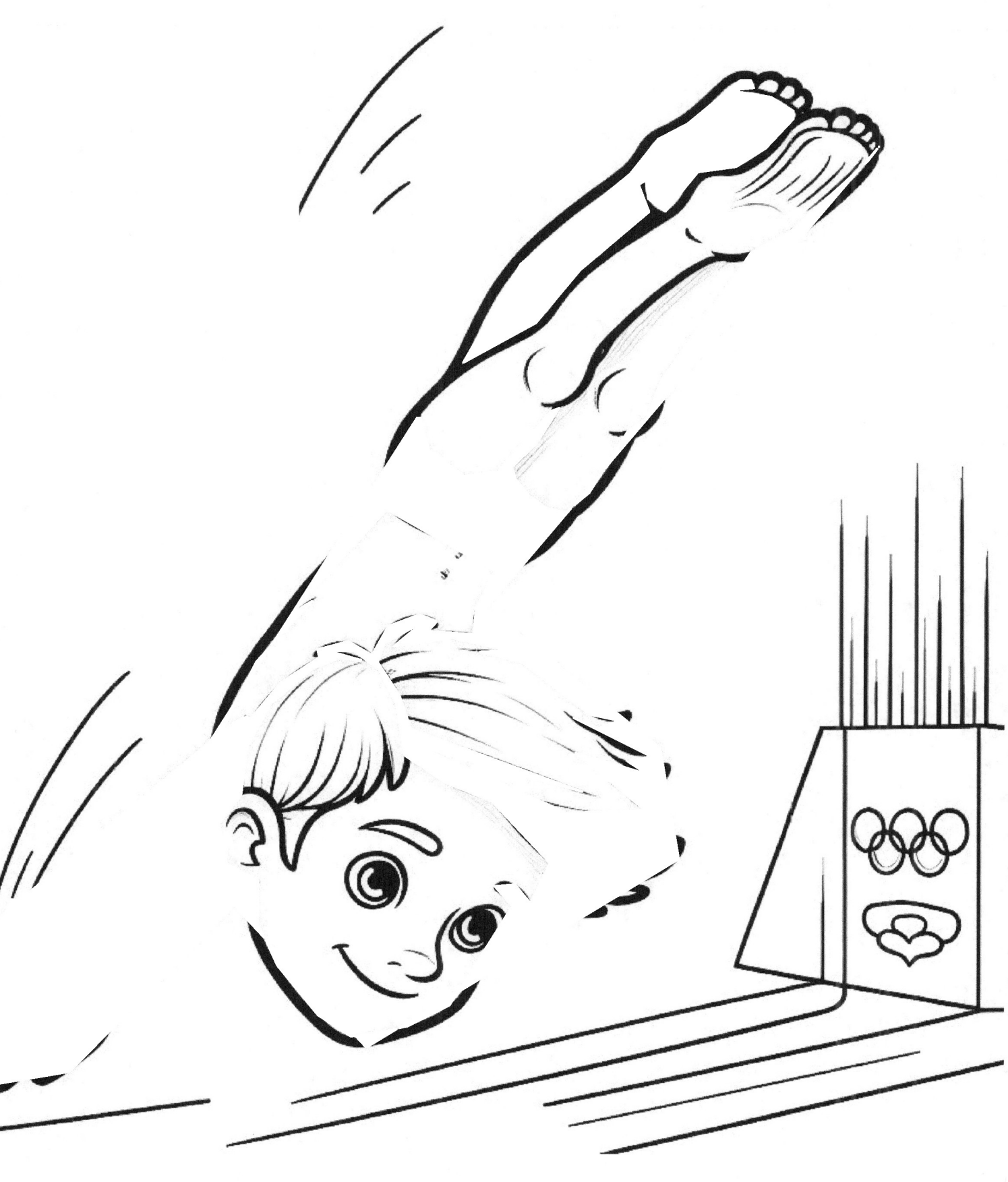

www.ingramcontent.com/pod-product-compliance
Lightning Source LLC
Chambersburg PA
CBHW062121220526
45471CB00010B/3821